OUTWARD BOUND
ROPES, KNOTS, AND HITCHES

SECOND EDITION

BUCK TILTON

FALCON

GUILFORD, CONNECTICUT

An imprint of The Rowman & Littlefield Publishing Group, Inc.
4501 Forbes Blvd., Ste. 200
Lanham, MD 20706
www.rowman.com

Falcon and FalconGuides are registered trademarks and Make Adventure Your Story is a trademark of The Rowman & Littlefield Publishing Group, Inc.

Distributed by NATIONAL BOOK NETWORK

British Library Cataloguing in Publication Information available

Library of Congress Cataloging-in-Publication Data available

ISBN 978-1-4930-3503-8 (paperback)
ISBN 978-1-4930-4798-7 (e-book)

∞™ The paper used in this publication meets the minimum requirements of American National Standard for Information Sciences—Permanence of Paper for Printed Library Materials, ANSI/NISO Z39.48-1992.

CONTENTS

Contents

Dear fellow adventurer:

Whether you're about to embark on your first outdoor experience or your twentieth; whether you're nervous or excited; whether you'll be backpacking, rock climbing, whitewater rafting, or sailing—no matter the recreation type— we believe the outdoors is the best classroom.

That's because we learn best through experience, challenge, adventure, and, most important, by being in a community of fellow compassionate people who will support us in these efforts. In the outdoors, we find common ground, a place to meet both physically and mentally. We strive together to meet a goal that seems out of reach on our own, but achievable when we work side by side, and through this experience, we see our true selves.

It's this power of community, of taking risks, of being uncomfortable, of saying "no" to mediocrity, of finding refuge from self-imposed limitations, that are our real reasons for adventure. These are the reasons why we'll wake up before dawn to canoe with the sunrise, why we'll backtrack four miles on tired feet after taking a wrong turn and sing the theme song to *Mission Impossible* to get through it, why we'll fight to stay awake just to stare at the stars in a deep black sky a little longer.

We hope this field guide will lead, motivate, and inspire you to learn new skills and master old ones, to challenge yourself and discover new passions, to strengthen your community, to uncover your deepest strengths, and to remember that it's not about the adventure—it's about every day after.

To serve, to strive, and not to yield.

Josh Brankman,
Executive Director, Outward Bound USA

ABOUT OUTWARD BOUND

Outward Bound USA celebrates more than fifty-five years of outdoor education programs that inspire people of all ages to enhance positive change in their communities and to create a more compassionate and resilient world for generations to come.

Outward Bound is globally recognized as the leading outdoor experiential education organization, annually serving close to fifty thousand youth and adults from communities across the United States.

At Outward Bound, we believe that values are best learned when experienced concretely rather than taught abstractly; that when the makeup of a crew crosses racial, economic, or religious lines, differences are celebrated, appreciated, and valued. Together, we seek, embrace, and value adventure and the lifelong pursuit of learning.

The National Network of Outward Bound Schools in the United States

There are eleven regional Outward Bound Schools that operate across the United States. Each School has autonomy to deliver Outward Bound courses in its region and to build strong ties within its local communities and with its regional school partners.

Each school develops programs that serve specific student populations or needs and programs that respond to issues directly affecting its local communities.

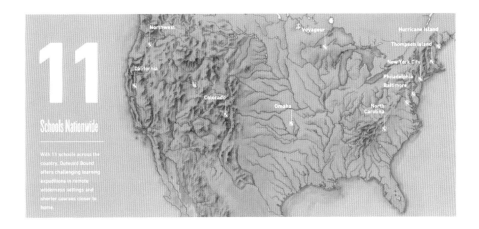

For many years, the Hurricane Outward Bound School has offered semester-long expeditions where learning at sea, from the Maine coast to the Florida Keys, becomes a formative part of a student's gap year plan. The Colorado Outward Bound School also offers semester-long courses where students begin their coursework in the Rocky Mountains of Colorado and conclude their coursework in Ecuador, one of the most biodiverse countries in the world. The Baltimore Chesapeake Bay Outward Bound School, for example, developed The Police Youth Challenge to address the deeply rooted and fraught relationships between police officers and young people across the city, and endeavors to connect them across issues and identities. The program has created positive, systemic change empowering young people and officers to see their leadership potential, to shape their sense of responsibility to their communities, and to act with compassion toward themselves and their neighbors.

While each school operates autonomously, they all benefit from OBUSA's national network, which ensures a high level of consistency in program quality, safety, and outcomes.

Outward Bound Learning Expeditions

Central to its mission are the values of inclusion and diversity, evidenced by its scholarship program designed to attract and benefit populations that are typically underserved. Approximately 45 percent of participants receive financial support, and they span ethnic, socioeconomic, and geographic diversity.

In the United States, to advance the mission of "changing lives through challenge and discovery" and to achieve our goals of developing compassionate, purposeful people, Outward Bound now offers its unique blend of adventure-based programming for a broad range of student populations including:

- Highly motivated teens and young adults
- Adults
- Veterans
- Professionals
- Outdoor educators
- Struggling teens and young adults
- Partnerships with schools and other youth-serving organizations

Although programs vary broadly in student populations served, location, and objective, they all contain elements that are central to the development of effective and compassionate citizens: adventure and challenge; learning through experience; integrity and excellence; inclusion and diversity; social and environmental responsibility; leadership and character development; and compassion and service.

OUTWARD BOUND INSTRUCTORS

Outward Bound instructors are highly trained and qualified educators and outdoor skills specialists. Participant safety is a high priority—foundational to every program. Every course is led by instructors who hold, at minimum, wilderness first-responder-level certifications and who have completed hundreds of hours of educational, safety, student, and activity-management training.

Instructors are proficient in and passionate about the specific wilderness skills of the activity they teach, whether rock climbing, sailing, mountaineering, sea kayaking, canoeing, or whitewater rafting. To help students along their personal growth paths, instructors are trained in managing groups and individuals. A vital component of every course is the instructor's ability to not only shepherd students through individual course challenges but also to help them work as effective leaders and contributing members of their team.

Outward Bound's Lasting Impact

The impact of each expedition extends well beyond the course itself. This impact is different for each student but can be seen in a variety of ways, including improved school performance, closer relationships with family and friends, or a new commitment to service.

When Outward Bound students return home, they bring with them a new sense of responsibility, an enhanced appreciation of the environment, and a strong service ethic that they share with friends, family, and their community.

INTRODUCTION

Looking back now over thousands of miles of trail and river, over hundreds of campsites, over the teaching I've done on Outward Bound courses from Maine to Florida, the list of skills offered by instructors to students seems endless: paddling a canoe, hoisting a sail, packing a pack, reading a map, treating a blister, picking a tent site, firing up a stove, cooking dinner—to name just a few. If, however, one skill stands out as universally useful, a skill you might use in any situation, in any environment, on any trip, it is the tying of knots.

Knots hold the outdoor world together. Properly tied, they prevent the boat from drifting away, the tent from lifting off in a high wind, and the bear from reaching the food bag. The right knot turns a length of rope into a clothesline, an anchor line, or a zip line. A good knot holds the sailing ship on course and the canoe to the top of the vehicle. A matter of life and death, the climber is secured to the rope and from falling off the end of the rope by knots.

To tie a knot is to add your name to a rich history. Long before mallet and peg, hammer and nail, glue, duct tape, or Velcro, there was cordage—and the knots that made it useful. Beside the unknown inventor of the wheel and the forgotten discoverer of fire making, I rank equally as a genius the man or woman who figured out how to entangle the ends of vines and plants' fibers in ways that would keep them from untangling. The tying of the first knot may have occurred more than 100,000 years ago. How else were prehistoric stone ax heads attached to prehistoric ax handles? No evidence, however, remains. But off the coast of Denmark, a fishhook was found still tied to a line (a length of sinew or gut) with what we know today as a clove hitch (see page 24). This hook-and-line was estimated at more than 10,000 years old. Part of a knotted fishing net retrieved from a bog in Finland has been dated circa 7200 BCE. During the zeniths of their civilizations, the Egyptians, Greeks, and Romans tied complex knots for diverse jobs—and left wonders that remain thousands of years later.

From the icebound polar regions to the ever-warm equatorial regions, all cultures in all times have knotted cords. Over the centuries knots have been used by builders, surveyors, soldiers, and sorcerers. The butcher, the miller, the cobbler, the farmer, the weaver, the housewife—they all needed a knot or two, or three. Knots were used for communication, for record keeping, in religious rites, and for corporal punishment.

It was at sea, though, under sail, that the science and art of knot tying reached its greatest extent. As the scope and practice of ships at sea expanded, so did the knots—in both form and function—which made seagoing ventures possible. Outward Bound, loaded with nautical tradition, carries on the history of the sea and the knot in sailing trips. (Still, it should be remembered, as Geoffrey Budworth writes in *The Illustrated Encyclopedia of Knots:* "For every knot tied aboard ship throughout the last millennium, another was tied ashore.")

An exhaustive compendium of knots would be a weighty tome indeed, including today more than 4,000 recognized ways of acceptably entrapping cordage. And that number does not include the variations possible with many knots. This book, of course, in no way pretends to be "complete" in the exhaustive sense. It does include seventy-three knots—more than enough to get every camping, climbing, and boating job done, whether on an Outward Bound course or off. Do you need to know them all? If not, which knots should you know?

Knots You Need

The International Guild of Knot Tyers (IGKT), founded in the United Kingdom in 1982, published in June of 1999 from their Surrey branch a list of six knots they think should be known first for use with modern rope. These are the figure 8 knot (see page 10), sheet bend (see page 14), bowline (see page 52), rolling hitch (see page 69), constrictor knot (see page 73), and the round turn and two half hitches (see page 86). They further suggested the figure 8 might be the best overall knot since it can be modified to serve as a stopper, bend, loop, or hitch (see Knot Terminology, page x). The "Surrey Six," however, despite its thoughtful creation, may not meet all of your knot needs.

You will need to explore knots, and tie lots, and choose the one or two (or more) that consistently meet the demands you place on them. But you are limited only by your willingness to learn. There are many knots fit to be tied.

Today's knots are most often tied by campers, boaters/sailors, and climbers. This book is divided into those three categories. But knots themselves do not divide neatly. The overhand knot, for example, falls easily into all three categories, as does the double overhand and the half hitch. The bowline, too, is useful in camping, climbing, and boating. The fisherman's knot is used by campers and climbers (as well as fishermen), and the sheet bend and double sheet bend could be useful in almost any situation. And it's always fun to tie a monkey's fist even if you don't need one.

Due to the lack of a neat division of knots into categories, I encourage you to read the entire book. As a camper, you may find the knot you have always wanted in the boating or climbing chapter. A boater's soon-to-be favorite knot might be found in the chapter on miscellaneous knots. And the quest for the perfect knot or knots is sure to be, as it always has been, an enjoyable journey.

Knot Terminology

The world of knotting has developed specific meanings for certain words and phrases. The end of the rope or cord used to tie a knot is the *working end,* and the other end is the *standing end.* In between the working and standing ends lies the *standing part.* When a section of cordage is doubled into a U shape, a *bight* is formed. A bight is the first step in many knots. When a section of cordage is doubled and crosses over itself, it becomes a *loop,* another start for numerous knots.

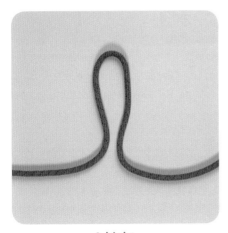

A bight.

A loop.

Where the rope or cord crosses itself is known as a *crossing point.* When the working end is not pulled completely through a knot, a *draw loop* is formed, which turns the working end into a quick-release device. A knot that comes undone or untied may also be said to *spill* or *capsize* (a reminder of the nautical history of knots). To take a wrap around a post or rail is to take a *turn,* but another half turn around the post or rail creates a *round turn.*

"Knot" itself can be a generic term applied to any interlacing of flexible material that involves a tucked end or a bight. But "knot" can also have a more

A draw loop.

A turn with the rope doubled.

A round turn.

A stopper knot.

A bend.

A hitch.

specific definition. It can be what ties two ends of the same line together, such as a bowknot in a shoelace, and "knot" typically refers to anything tied in small stuff, such as twine or string.

A *stopper* is tied into the end of a rope to prevent it from slipping through a slit or hole, or to prevent the end of rope from fraying. Stoppers are sometimes tied as simple backups for more complex knots to keep the complex knots from spilling. A *bend* is a joining knot, one that joins or "bends" two separate ropes or cords together to form one rope or cord. A *hitch* is used to attach a rope to a post, pile, ring, rail, another line, or even to itself—or to attach something to a rope.

Knot Nomenclature

Some knots have survived for ages without ever being given an official title, while others are tagged with an unruly list of names. The fisherman's knot, for example, may also be known as the angler's knot, halibut knot, water knot, waterman's knot, English knot, Englishman's knot, or true lover's knot. Additional names for a knot, furthermore, may be unclear. A double fisherman's knot is sometimes called the grinner knot, but "grinner" has been applied to other knots as well.

A knot's name may also reflect what it looks like. A figure 8 knot looks like its name, and so does a round turn and two half hitches. Some knots are named for their inventors: Ashley's stopper and the prusik, for instance. Some knots are named for their uses: hangman's noose, constrictor knot, cow hitch. And knot names are often misleading. A fisherman's knot is used as a bend; a fisherman's bend is actually a hitch; a midshipman's hitch is really a loop; and a girth hitch is also known as a ring bend—well, you get the picture. As a final confusing act, occasionally two different knots will bear the same name. The water knot, when referring to the fisherman's knot, isn't the same knot as the water knot when referring to the climbing knot. In the end the naming of knots is, for the most part, a rather haphazard affair.

Knot-Tying Tips

Choose the simplest knot that will get the job done. It will be easiest to learn, easiest to remember, quickest to tie, and usually the easiest to untie.

Practice in order to tie all knots correctly. Many knots can be tied more than one way. The route seldom matters, but the final configuration is of the utmost importance. A tuck in the wrong direction, for instance, turns a square (reef) knot into an indefensible granny knot.

Knots can be tied right-handed or left-handed, depending on the dominant hand of the tyer. A knot tied right-handed will be the mirror image of the same knot tied left-handed, and they both will work. (A few knots have a right-handed element and a left-handed element.)

A properly tied knot must be properly tightened. Most knots must be slowly tightened—shaped, kneaded, molded, coaxed—into proper configuration, which almost always means there are no gaps in the knot, no places where light can pass through. It is rarely a matter of tugging on the working and standing ends.

When tightening any knot, follow this guideline: Work snug and then tighten. Take out the slack a little at a time, removing it from both the working and the standing ends. Last of all, give it a tightening tug.

Choose the best cordage for the job. A knot works only as well as the rope or cord of which it is made. Highly elastic cords, such as bungees, shed a bowline (see page 52), but a vice versa (see page 46) holds securely. It is, in other words, not only a matter of the right knot but also the right material to tie it in (see Of Ropes and Cordage, page 1).

Disclaimers

In order to achieve the maximum photographic effect, the text may refer to one type of cord or line while the photographs show another. Trust the text for information, and trust the photo sequences for the proper knot-tying steps.

It is suggested in several places in this book that a specific knot will work, if tied correctly, to save or help save a life. This occurs almost exclusively in the climbing-knot chapters. The use of knots in this book to save or help save a life, however, should only be undertaken by people qualified to use the knots appropriately. This is not a how-to book for activities other than the tying of knots themselves.

OF ROPES AND CORDAGE

For a knot to exist, something in which to tie the knot must first exist. Traditionally, if that something is more than 10 millimeters in diameter, it is called rope. Ropes for special purposes are called lines—stern line, tow line, clothesline. Smaller stuff is often referred to as "smaller stuff," an informal title, and includes cord (which usually refers to large smaller stuff) and then twine or string (and perhaps thread). The smaller stuff is further set apart by its diameter: 5-millimeter cord, 6-millimeter cord, and so forth. None of these terms are sacred. Fishing line, for instance, no matter how remarkably thin, is always called line, and the word "cordage" may be used to describe both ropes and cords.

The first cordage came from plant and animal fibers. Flax and jute are made from plant stems. Hemp and manila come from plant leaves, and cotton from seeds. Ropes have been created from coconut shell fibers, grass, wool, silk, and hair from horses, camels, and even humans. Excellent cordage has also been made from leather.

Since natural fibers are limited in length to a maximum of about 3 feet, ropes woven from natural fibers are always relatively weak. They also swell when wet, freeze and crack in extreme cold, provide something interesting for insects and rodents to chew on, and require tedious drying before storing. The ends of the fibers stick out from the surface of the cordage, making them rough on the hands of the handlers. All things considered, the development of synthetic fibers was a glorious advance.

Ropes and cordage today are manufactured almost exclusively from nylon, which was introduced to the domestic market in 1938, and from other more recently developed synthetic fibers with names such as polyester, polypropylene and polyethylene. These fibers run continuously along the length of a rope. In addition to being phenomenally stronger and lighter than natural fibers, synthetics handle easier, last longer, and resist abrasion, rot, and mildew. Some of them (polypropylene ropes, for instance) float as well. Please note that nylon ropes, despite their advantages, will absorb water, thereby losing some strength, and will sink in a sea. In a canoe, a floating rope might be a good idea. While climbing, a stronger, more supple rope might be a better choice. Being smooth on the surface, they are also easy on the hands. Important on the list of benefits, synthetic fibers stretch when the load is applied, sometimes up to 40 percent, and return to their original length when the load is off.

When stretch is not relevant but great strength is, Kevlar ropes, stronger than steel, top the list. And synthetics can be made in a wide range of colors, from subtle to brilliant. When ropes are arranged close together yet do different jobs, as happens sometimes in climbing, different colors make life easier as well as safer.

Synthetics do have their negative aspects, though. They melt if high heat is applied. Even high friction-generated heat will harden the surface of a synthetic rope, making it less functional. Knots tend to stay tied in "hairy" ropes of natural fibers, but knots tied in synthetics tend to fall apart more often due to the smoothness of the ropes. This has led to the use of backup knots (simpler knots preventing more complex knots from slipping) and the evolution of new knots that are more secure in synthetics.

The making of most synthetic cordage begins with long monofilaments, although sometimes multifilaments (a cluster of very thin fibers) are used. Batches of the filaments are spun together clockwise to make long yarns.

To make a *laid rope* (laid in strands), a batch of the clockwise-spun yarns are spun together counterclockwise to make a strand. When the required size of strand is reached, three strands are spun together, clockwise again this time, to make the traditional three-stranded rope. It is all the spinning and counter-spinning during the manufacturing process that causes the strands of a rope to cling tightly together.

More often synthetic cordage is *braided* rather than laid. Most braided ropes are made of two layers, a sheath and a core. The sheath consists of interwoven yarns that protectively enclose the core. The core yarns often run parallel to the length of the rope but may be laid or even plaited (interwoven) if a very large and strong rope is needed. (This sheath-and-core construction is typically called *kernmantle* by climbers.) Occasionally braided ropes consist of three layers: outer sheath, inner sheath, and core.

All cordage, whether laid or braided, may be manufactured with the fibers under high tension and called *hard-laid,* or made with the fibers under less tension and known as *soft-laid.* Hard-laid ropes are more durable but also more stiff, especially when new.

A critical aspect of managing rope, no matter what material it is made of, concerns the ends. When the ends are cut, the rope gradually falls apart. Synthetics, lacking the inner cohesiveness of the fibers, fall apart faster than natural fiber ropes. The solution: Do not cut any cordage without first taking steps to prevent unraveling and fraying. There are numerous ways to accomplish this.

Whipping (see page 116) and *splicing* (see pages 113 and 114) were once commonly used and still work to prevent a rope from unraveling. Liquid whipping, a manufactured product into which rope ends are dipped, is also available. Three-stranded rope ends can be temporarily protected with a constrictor knot (see page 73) tied in twine around the end, or with tape. With synthetic cordage, cutting with a heated knife heat-seals the cut ends. Heat-sealed ends that will see hard use are best backed up with tape or another method of protection against deconstruction.

Rope Strength vs. Knot Strength

The breaking strength of a rope or cord, determined by the manufacturer, tells how much stress or weight that rope or cord will bear before breaking. Knot strength refers to how much the knot reduces the breaking strength of a rope compared to the breaking strength of the same rope unknotted. Any rope or cord is strongest when stressed or loaded in a straight line. Any turn reduces strength, and knots turn, twist, nip, and tuck cordage from gentle curves to sharp angles. Therefore, knots vary in strength as ropes vary in strength.

The measurement of knot strength, unfortunately, is far from a precise science. It is generally accepted that the overhand knot (see page 6), perhaps the weakest knot, reduces the breaking strength of a rope by more than one-half. So the overhand knot is often said to be 45 percent efficient, or in other words, the overhand knot's strength is 45 percent (which means the breaking strength of the rope is reduced by 55 percent).

It should be remembered that a slow and steady pull challenges a rope's breaking strength far less than a sudden shock load. Only the strongest knots should be used if a rope might be shock-loaded (such as when a climber falls). Also, remember that a knot tied properly is stronger than a knot tied improperly. Or as the old adage explains: "A not neat knot need not be knotted."

With relativity in mind, the figure 8 knot (see page 10), the variations on the figure 8, the clove hitch (see page 24), the double bowline (see page 56), and the round turn and two half hitches (see page 86) are considered very strong knots. The girth hitch (see page 81), the double fisherman's knot (see page 90), and the water knot (see page 92) are strong knots. By comparison, a sheepshank knot (see page 112) should never be found in ropes of vital importance.

Be not dismayed, however. Although this book does address knot strength when it seems relevant, modern synthetic ropes and cords are so incredibly strong that they are not often significantly threatened by knots.

Knot Security

A strong knot is not necessarily a secure knot. Knot security is a different consideration than knot strength. A knot that can be shaken loose to spill of its own accord, such as the bowline (see page 52), is an insecure knot. A knot that slips gradually due to intermittent stresses, such as the clove hitch (see page 24), is an insecure knot. A knot such as the killick hitch (see page 38) may be insecure when pulled in one direction but secure when pulled in the opposite direction. And a knot that holds well in all conditions and in wet, slimy, slippery rope or cord is a secure knot. The vice versa (see page 46) is an example of a secure and strong knot. This book addresses knot security when it is deemed relevant.

Clove Hitch on a stake backed up with an Overhand Draw Loop.

CAMPING KNOTS:
Stoppers

Overhand Knot

A SIMPLE AND USEFUL STOPPER KNOT THAT ALSO FORMS THE BASIS FOR MANY INTRICATE KNOTS

As the most fundamental knot, the overhand stands alone as the knot first learned, often by accident, by anyone who handles rope or cordage of any type. A small stopper, it may not meet the demands of all situations. The overhand is repeated time and time again as part of other knots. Since this knot reduces the strength of a rope by as much as 55 percent, remove unwanted overhands from the middle of ropes as soon as possible.

Overhand Knot: Step 1

Create a loop in the working end of a rope or cord.

Overhand Knot: Step 2

Take the working end over the standing part and back up through the loop. Tighten the knot by pulling simultaneously on the working end and the standing end.

Overhand Knot with Draw Loop

A VARIATION OF THE OVERHAND KNOT THAT IS SLIGHTLY LARGER AND MUCH EASIER TO UNTIE

When a basic overhand knot is tightened over a loop, the loop may be drawn out with relative ease by holding the knot and pulling on the working end. This makes the overhand knot with draw loop a better choice than the basic overhand when the knot will be untied soon or often.

Overhand Knot with Draw Loop: Step 1

Tie an overhand knot (see page 5) in the working end of a rope or cord.

Overhand Knot with Draw Loop: Step 2

Before tightening the knot, take the working end back through the overhand. Tighten the knot by pulling on the loop with one hand and the working end and standing part with the other hand.

7

Heaving Line Knot

A LARGE STOPPER KNOT THAT ADDS CONSIDERABLE WEIGHT TO THE END OF A ROPE

The weight of the heaving line knot makes it useful for throwing the end of a rope over a greater distance. Tossing the end of a rope intended for hanging a bear bag over the limb of a tree, for instance, is easier with this knot. When a heavy rope needs to be strung across a gap, the heaving line knot can be tied in the end of a lighter line, which in turn is then tied to the heavier line. The lighter line is thrown more easily over the gap,

Heaving Line Knot: Step 1

Form a loop in the working end of a rope. Bring the working end over the standing part and back under the loop.

Heaving Line Knot: Step 2

Bring the working end back over the loop, compressing the loop.

and the heavier line then is drawn (or heaved) behind it. When sailors need to toss a rope between ship and dock, the heaving line knot works well. Its other name, the monk's knot, refers to its use by Franciscan monks to weight the ends of the cords they used as belts. In addition to being useful in camping and boating, the heaving line knot is sometimes employed by climbers.

Heaving Line Knot: Step 3

Make three more turns with the working end around the loop.

Heaving Line Knot: Step 4

After the final turn bring the working end through the loop, holding the turns around the loop as tight as possible. Tighten the knot by pulling on the working end and the standing part. As the turns tighten, form the knot into its final shape.

Figure 8 Knot

A QUICK, EFFICIENT,
AND ATTRACTIVE STOPPER KNOT

The figure 8 knot is one of the fundamental knots. However, despite its bulkier appearance, it does not stop a rope from running through a hole or slot any better than a basic overhand. What it does do is untie easier than an overhand, and so it works well when a stopper needs to be tied and untied often. An ancient knot, known since ships first sailed out of sight of shore, its characteristic figure 8 shape also signifies faithful love in heraldry, showing up in numerous coats of arms, where it

Figure 8 Knot: Step 1	Figure 8 Knot: Step 2

Form a loop in the working end of a rope.	**Twist the end of the loop to form a second loop.**

has been given other names, including the Flemish knot and the Savoy knot. The figure 8 forms the basis for many other knots and is, therefore, a knot one needs to know. It can be modified to serve as a bend, loop, or hitch, and it has been dubbed by the International Guild of Knot Tyers as the best overall knot.

Figure 8 Knot: Step 3

Bring the working end of the rope up through the second loop.

Figure 8 Knot: Step 4

Tighten the knot by pulling on both the working end and the standing part. Notice the characteristic figure 8 shape that gives this knot its name.

Figure 8 Knot with Draw Loop

A VARIATION OF THE FIGURE 8 KNOT
THAT IS MUCH EASIER TO UNTIE

When a stopper knot will see only temporary use, the figure 8 with draw loop makes an excellent choice. This knot releases quickly, as any draw loop does, by pulling on the working end. The addition of the draw loop increases the size of the standard figure 8 if a larger stopper is needed. A favorite in synthetic ropes, figure 8 knots, even this one with a draw loop, may jam in wet ropes of natural fibers. This knot is useful to climbers and boaters as well as campers.

Figure 8 Knot with Draw Loop:
Step 1

Create a figure 8 knot (see page 9) in the working end of a rope, but do not tighten the knot.

Figure 8 Knot with Draw Loop:
Step 2

Bring the working end back through the upper loop of the figure 8 but only far enough to form the draw loop. Tighten the knot by pulling on the loop and the standing part.

Square (Reef) Knot

A QUICK AND SIMPLE BEND FOR TYING TOGETHER TWO ROPES OR CORDS OF EQUAL DIAMETER

This fundamental knot, known to many as the square knot, is more accurately called the reef knot. It is used for binding two pieces of cordage of equal diameter or two ends of the same piece of cordage. If improperly tied, as it often is, it becomes the infamous and highly insecure granny knot. Even tied correctly, the square knot loosens easily and should not be used as a bend where security is required. Knot tyers involved in many different pursuits use this one.

Square Knot: Step 1	Square Knot: Step 2

Bring the two working ends of the two pieces of cordage together and cross them left over right.	Cross the two working ends a second time, right over left. Tighten by pulling simultaneously on both working ends and both standing parts.

Sheet Bend

A QUICK AND SIMPLE BEND FOR TYING TOGETHER TWO ROPES OR CORDS OF EQUAL OR UNEQUAL DIAMETER

Another fundamental knot and arguably the most commonly used bend, the sheet bend works well in lines of unequal diameter. The strength of this knot, however, decreases in direct proportion to the difference in the diameter of the lines joined. If the ropes are unequal in diameter, make the bight in the larger rope, and it will be more secure if both working ends emerge on the same side of the knot.

Sheet Bend: Step 1

Create a bight (see page xi) in the working end of one of the two ropes.

Sheet Bend: Step 2

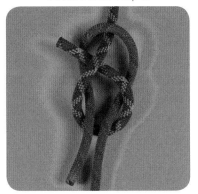

Bring the working end of the second rope through the bight, then around the back of the bight and across the top of the bight. Then bring it underneath itself and over the other rope, as shown in the photograph. Tighten by pulling on both standing parts.

Double Sheet Bend

A REINFORCED VERSION OF THE SHEET BEND THAT PROVIDES GREATER SECURITY

In uses where the basic sheet bend will tend to slip or entirely spill, the double sheet bend creates a more secure knot, even when the ropes are wet and even when the load is heavy. This is especially true when the ropes are of unequal diameter. Due to its greater security, the double sheet bend sees frequent use on boats and ships as well as in camp.

Double Sheet Bend: Step 1

Tie two ropes together with a sheet bend (see page 14).

Double Sheet Bend: Step 2

Bring the working end of the second rope around the bight in the first rope a second time before tucking it under itself, as shown in the final, upper photograph. Be sure the turns lie neatly beside each other before tightening.

Figure 8 Loop

A STRONG AND SECURE FIXED LOOP
FOR ALL DIAMETERS OF MATERIAL

The figure 8 loop is one of the most widely known and used loops. A well-liked camping knot, it is also popular with climbers and sometimes used by boaters. Once better known as the Flemish loop, this knot is tied on a bight and, therefore, may also be called the figure 8 on a bight. Since this knot is tied with the rope doubled, the characteristic figure 8 shape is actually a double figure 8, giving the figure 8 loop yet another name: the double figure 8 loop.

Figure 8 Loop: Step 1	Figure 8 Loop: Step 2

Create a large bight in the working end and double it over to form a loop.	Bring the doubled working end over the doubled standing part.

Whatever the name, it ties with relative ease and works well in diameters of cordage ranging from fine thread to thick rope. It also ranks high as a secure loop: Once tied, it stays tied. Even so, knot experts argue over whether or not the figure 8 loop should be finished with a stopper knot in the working end, a procedure that would eliminate any chance the figure 8 could slip. A stopper can be added with ease if the working end is left long enough. Those who argue against the stopper point out that the figure 8 loop, after being weighted, often proves difficult, but not impossible, to undo.

Figure 8 Loop: Step 3	Figure 8 Loop: Step 4
	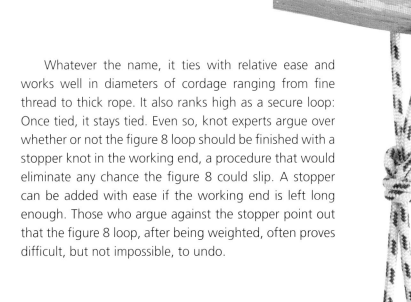
Bring the doubled working end up through the original loop.	**Tighten slowly by pulling on the loop and the main standing part to create the characteristic figure 8.**

Overhand Loop

A SIMPLE AND SECURE FIXED LOOP
FOR USE WITH STRING OR LIGHT CORD

Almost as simple as the basic overhand knot (see page 6), the overhand loop creates a quick and useful knot. This knot can be tied in the middle of a rope if a loop is needed there. It also offers another advantage: If a rope has a worn or weak point, the point can be incorporated into the loop, making the rope stronger. But be warned: This knot can jam when used in rope. Prevent jamming by keeping the knot from being too heavily loaded, especially shock loaded.

Overhand Loop: Step 1	Overhand Loop: Step 2

Make a relatively long bight in the working end of the cord.	**Tie an overhand knot (see page 6) with the doubled cord.**

Slipknot (Simple Noose)

THE SIMPLEST OF SLIDING LOOPS
THAT TIGHTENS WHEN PULLED

The slipknot, also known as the simple noose, can be tied in any type of cordage material, be it synthetic or natural fiber. It works well as the start of a lashing (when cordage is used to tie two or more objects, such as sticks or poles, together). Although included with camping knots, this one may be useful to climbers and boaters too. This knot appears to be an overhand with a draw loop. However, in an overhand with draw loop, the working end forms the loop. In a slipknot the standing part forms the loop.

Slipknot: Step 1	Slipknot: Step 2
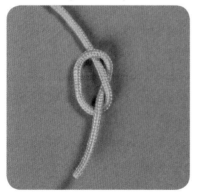	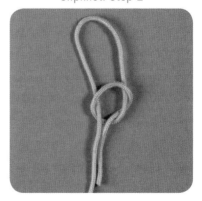
Tie an overhand knot (see page 6) near the working end of a rope or cord.	Pull the standing part up, over, and through the loop of the overhand knot. Tighten by pulling simultaneously on the loop created in the standing part and the working end.

Hangman's Knot (Noose)

AN EXTREMELY STRONG AND SECURE
SLIDING LOOP FOR HEAVY WEIGHTS
AND SUDDEN LOADS

The most notorious sliding loop of all time, the hangman's knot, or noose, is able to support very heavy weights and the hard jerk when a large load is suddenly applied. Even with heavy use, the noose unties—but not always with great ease. It does not actually slide with great ease either, and the more turns of the rope around itself during tying, the less easily it slides.

Hangman's Knot: Step 1

Form two bights in the working end of the rope, as shown in the photograph.

Hangman's Knot: Step 2

Bring the working end under both standing parts.

More than 400 years of history in which this knot has seen use suggest that the number of turns should be odd and usually between seven and thirteen, with thirteen being considered appropriate at an official, court-ordered hanging. Today, as in the past, the loop is typically adjusted to the desired size prior to weighting the rope. *Note:* This knot is sometimes used by boaters to secure a thimble (a "hard-eye") to the end of a rope without splicing.

Hangman's Knot: Step 3

Begin to make tight turns with the working end around both standing parts, moving from the bottom bight toward the top bight. Make between six and eight turns.

Hangman's Knot: Step 4

Leave enough of the working end to pull it through the last (uppermost) loop. Tighten by pulling on the lower loop.

CAMPING KNOTS:
Stationary Hitches

Half Hitch

THE SIMPLEST AND MOST WIDELY USED HITCH

Although not very secure, the half hitch quickly fastens a rope to a rail, bar, post, ring, or other object. Despite its name, this is actually a complete hitch, often used in the working end of a rope to back up and secure another knot that has already been tied. It is seen most often as part of a more complicated knot, but it can be used alone for simple jobs that do not require the knot to support much weight (such as hanging a small food bag out of reach of mice).

Half Hitch: Step 1

Drape the working end over or through the object to which the rope will be fastened.

Half Hitch: Step 2

Bring the working end back out and over the standing part and then through the loop created. Tighten by pulling simultaneously on the working end and standing part.

Two Half Hitches

AN ADVANCED VARIATION OF THE HALF HITCH THAT CREATES A MORE SECURE KNOT

Two half hitches bind a rope to an object or another rope with twice the security of a single half hitch. Security is lost, however, if the load is not applied at a right angle to the object. The knot is a half hitch tied on top of a half hitch. It does not have to be constantly loaded, but when it is, the load needs to be constant, or else it will work loose. A favorite among campers, two half hitches may be useful in climbing and boating.

Two Half Hitches: Step 1

Fasten a rope to an object with a half hitch (see page 22). Tighten the half hitch.

Two Half Hitches: Step 2

Take the working end around again, over the standing part again, and through the loop a second time. Tighten by pulling simultaneously on the working end and the standing part.

23

Clove Hitch

ONE OF THE BEST KNOWN AND MOST WIDELY USED GENERAL HITCHES

The simple beauty of the clove hitch, another fundamental knot, and the ability to tie it with one hand (with only a little practice), are offset by the fact that it works loose over time, especially if the pull on the rope is not at a right angle to the point of attachment. With that in mind, this knot is still one of the most universally useful of all quick hitches in all kinds of pursuits.

Clove Hitch: Step 1

Wrap the working end of the rope around an object, laying it over the standing part as shown in the photograph.

Clove Hitch: Step 2

Wrap the working end around the object a second time and underneath the crossed-over section of the first turn. Tighten by pulling simultaneously on the working end and standing end, taking care to keep the distinctive shape of the knot.

Clove Hitch on a Stake

A VARIATION OF THE CLOVE HITCH USED FOR TYING A ROPE TO A STAKE

This method of tying a clove hitch requires two hands but allows the rope to be dropped quickly over a stake or post instead of tying the knot around the object. As a bonus, it can be tied at any point in a rope—such as in the middle of 50 meters of cord. An ancient knot, the clove hitch is at least 10,000 years old (see Introduction). When a quick hitch is needed, climbers and boaters as well as campers use this knot.

Clove Hitch on a Stake: Step 1

Form two loops in a rope, one in the right hand, one in the left, as shown in the photograph.

Clove Hitch on a Stake: Step 2

Place the right-hand loop on top of the left-hand loop. Drop the two loops over a stake and tighten by pulling simultaneously on both ends of the rope, taking care to maintain the distinctive shape of the hitch.

25

Clove Hitch on a Ring

A VARIATION OF THE CLOVE HITCH USED FOR TYING A ROPE TO A RING

This method of tying a clove hitch to a ring or similar object allows the knot to be easily loosened and retightened to control the length of the rope leading to the ring. It is commonly used by anyone in just about any circumstance who needs a quick, temporary hitch.

Clove Hitch on a Ring: Step 1

Feed the working end of the rope through the ring from behind and bring it down and behind the standing part.

Clove Hitch on a Ring: Step 2

Bring the working end up through the ring again (from the back) and down through the back of the bight of the knot, as shown in the photograph. Tighten by pulling on the standing part.

Cow Hitch (Simple)

ANOTHER QUICK AND SIMPLE, THOUGH INSECURE, GENERAL-PURPOSE HITCH

The simple or common cow hitch, scoffed at by many knot enthusiasts, loosens easily due to the fact that the weight of a load pulls entirely on the standing part of the rope. It is often used to temporarily tether animals, but it should not be trusted for any length of time. Archaeological evidence shows that this knot has been around for centuries and deserves a place in knot literature. It will endure due to its simplicity.

Cow Hitch (Simple): Step 1

Drape the working end of a rope through a ring, as shown in the photograph, or over a rail or bar.

Cow Hitch (Simple): Step 2

Bring the working end across the front of the standing part, back up and through the ring or over the rail again, and down through the bight of the knot, as shown in the photograph. Tighten by pulling on the standing part.

27

Cow Hitch (Pedigree)

A VARIATION OF THE SIMPLE COW HITCH THAT CREATES A RELIABLE KNOT

By tucking the working end of the rope back into the simple cow hitch (see page 27), the pedigree cow hitch is created. That one tuck turns a lightweight and undependable knot into a fairly secure and serviceable knot with numerous uses. And, unlike the simple cow hitch, a load can be applied to the pedigree cow hitch from any angle, making it close to ideal for tethering a cow—or, for that matter, just about any animal.

Cow Hitch (Pedigree): Step 1

Drape the working end of a rope over a rail or bar, as shown in the photograph.

Cow Hitch (Pedigree): Step 2

Bring the working end across the front of the standing part.

It is a handy knot for suspending tools or other items from pegs or cross beams over patios or in garages, sheds, or other storage areas. It also works well as a starting point for lashings. The pedigree cow hitch is credited to Dr. Harry Asher and his 1989 publication, *The Alternative Knot Book.* (Dr. Asher, a founding member of the International Guild of Knot Tyers, also wrote about the theory behind why knots work.)

Cow Hitch (Pedigree): Step 3

Bring the working end back up and over the rail again, and down through the bight of the knot, as shown in the photograph.

Cow Hitch (Pedigree): Step 4

Tuck the working end behind both turns of the rope that go around the rail or bar. Tighten by pulling on the standing part.

29

Bull Hitch

AN EVEN STRONGER, "BEEFIER" VARIATION ON THE COW HITCH

The bull hitch offers better security than both the cow hitch (see page 27) and the pedigree cow hitch (see page 28). It is, however, a bit more complex than those knots. Because the bull hitch tends to jam if the standing part is heavily loaded, especially by a sudden jerk, it is most often used as a temporary tether and not in situations where it will be left unguarded for a long time. A new binding in knot literature, the bull hitch first appeared in print in the

Bull Hitch: Step 1	Bull Hitch: Step 2

Drape the working end of a rope over a rail or bar and bring it across the front of the standing part.	Wrap the working end in a complete turn around the standing part of the rope.

January 1995 edition of *Knotting Matters,* the newsletter of the International Guild of Knot Tyers. It is credited to Robert Pont, a member of the guild.

Bull Hitch: Step 3

Bring the working end up and over the rail or bar (from the back) a second time (as shown in the photograph).

Bull Hitch: Step 4

Take the working end down through the loop in the knot through which the standing part passes. Tighten by pulling on the standing part.

31

Transom Knot

A USEFUL KNOT FOR TYING TOGETHER TWO CROSSED PIECES OF RIGID MATERIAL

Back when lashing was more popular in camping, when limbs of trees were freely lopped off and tied together as frames for tents and tarps, the transom knot (called by some the strangle knot) found many uses. It is still a handy knot, useful for securing a pole between two trees from which gear may be hung or to which the high end of a tarp may be attached for shelter.

Survival courses often include this knot as a means to aid in the construction of primitive shelters. It works well in light cord to bind together light pieces of wood, such as

Transom Knot: Step 1	Transom Knot: Step 2

With the working end of the rope, make a loop around the vertical piece of rigid material.	Take the working end across the horizontal piece of rigid material and completely around the vertical piece below the horizontal piece, as shown in the photograph.

when a kite or garden trellis is assembled, and it holds nicely in synthetic or natural fiber cord. It is similar to but slightly less complex than the constrictor knot (see page 73). This knot is typically tied in short pieces of rope or cordage, since longer pieces are unwieldy and unnecessary to get the job done.

Transom Knot: Step 3

Cross the horizontal piece a second time. Take the working end underneath itself where it crosses the horizontal piece.

Transom Knot: Step 4

Take the working end underneath the standing part where it forms part of the original loop (as shown in the photograph) and tighten by pulling on both ends of the rope.

Trucker's Hitch

A KNOT THAT PROVIDES LEVERAGE TO TAKE UP SLACK IN A ROPE OR CORD

The trucker's hitch (sometimes known as the cinch knot or power cinch) is more accurately described as a system of knots giving a three-to-one mechanical advantage that allows tension to be created in a rope or cord. This knot, in other words, works like a pulley, allowing more tension to be created than by simply pulling on the end of the rope. A rope can be drawn as tight as a guitar string, if needed, but the amount of tension is under the control of the knot tyer.

Trucker's Hitch: Step 1

First, tie a quick-release loop, such as an overhand loop (see page 18), an appropriate distance from the working end of the rope or cord. Then pass the working end through the tie-down point (a ring in the photograph, for example).

Trucker's Hitch: Step 2

Bring the working end through the quick-release loop.

This knot is an excellent method of keeping a tent line taut between the tent and an anchor or for tying a tight line between two trees from which a bear bag can be hung. It also works well for securing gear or a canoe to the top of a vehicle. Once learned, campers—and climbers and boaters—tend to wonder how they ever got along without the trucker's hitch.

Trucker's Hitch: Step 3

Pull the working end toward the tie-down point to create the amount of tension required.

Trucker's Hitch: Step 4

When appropriate tension is in the rope or cord, secure the knot with a half hitch (see page 22), or an overhand with draw loop (see page 7), as shown in the photograph.

Tautline Hitch

THIS KNOT PROVIDES LEVERAGE TO TAKE UP SLACK IN A ROPE OR CORD

Like the trucker's hitch (see page 34), the tautline hitch creates a tight (or taut) line but does so with a simple knot instead of a system of knots. Because it is simpler than the trucker's hitch, it is often taught to beginning knot tyers as a method of creating tension, as in a tent line. The knot slides freely but jams against the rope or cord it is tied around when a load is applied. Far more tension can be created with a trucker's hitch, and the trucker's hitch is more secure, so most knot tyers eventually leave

Tautline Hitch: Step 1

Take the working end around or through a secure or tie-down point (such as the ring in the photograph) and back under the standing part to form a loop.

Tautline Hitch: Step 2

With the working end, make two or three turns around the standing part within the loop, as shown in the photograph.

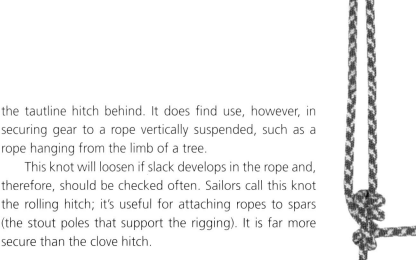

the tautline hitch behind. It does find use, however, in securing gear to a rope vertically suspended, such as a rope hanging from the limb of a tree.

This knot will loosen if slack develops in the rope and, therefore, should be checked often. Sailors call this knot the rolling hitch; it's useful for attaching ropes to spars (the stout poles that support the rigging). It is far more secure than the clove hitch.

Tautline Hitch: Step 3

Bring the working end down and underneath the standing part outside the loop, as shown in the photograph, forming a second loop.

Tautline Hitch: Step 4

Take the working end through the second loop and tighten by pulling on the standing part. The knot can now be pushed up the standing part, taking slack out of the rope. Under pressure, the knot grips and holds against the standing part, maintaining tension in the rope.

Timber Hitch

TEMPORARILY ATTACHES A ROPE TO AN OBJECT FOR DRAGGING, RAISING, OR LOWERING

A fundamental knot, the timber hitch serves as a short-term noose, quickly tying a rope to a heavy object that needs to be moved by pulling, dragging, lifting, or lowering. It is very secure under tension and never jams. But be careful: Those new to knots often tie this one incorrectly, and then the knot fails. The timber hitch can also loosen and fail if there is too much slack in the rope or erratic pulling on the rope.

Timber Hitch: Step 1	Timber Hitch: Step 2

Pass the working end around the object to be moved and then behind and around the standing part.	Twist the working end around itself (not around the standing part) at least three times. The number of twists can be increased to boost the grip of the knot, depending on the size and weight of the object. Tighten by pulling on the standing part.

38

Killick Hitch

A VARIATION OF THE TIMBER HITCH THAT PROVIDES MORE SECURITY

When moving a heavy object, especially by dragging or towing (even through water), the killick hitch (a timber hitch with an additional half hitch) creates a more secure bond between rope and object. Sometimes called the kelleg hitch, this knot works well if the object to be moved is long. Small boats sometimes use this hitch to attach oddly shaped and heavy objects to the boat as an anchor.

Killick Hitch: Step 1	Killick Hitch: Step 2
	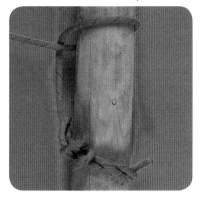
Tie a timber hitch (see page 38) around the object to be moved.	At some distance down the rope, add a half hitch around the object, as shown in the photograph.

Mooring line.

Braided rope.

Double Overhand Knot

A COMPACT STOPPER FOR SMALL- TO LARGE-DIAMETER CORD OR LINE

Not only a simple and useful stopper knot, the double overhand works in all sizes of material, from thin thread to thick cord. It shows up as a basis for other knots, including bends, and can be tied in the end of lines to prevent fraying. You will find it useful in activities other than boating. It is an essential knot to know.

Double Overhand Knot: Step 1

Tie an overhand knot (see page 6) in the working end.

Double Overhand Knot: Step 2

Tuck the working end through the loop of the overhand a second time. Tighten by pulling gently on both ends. As the knot begins to tighten, twist both ends of the knot in opposite directions with your fingers. Continue to tighten to give the knot its characteristic shape.

Ashley's Stopper Knot

A BULKY STOPPER TO BLOCK HOLES OR SLOTS WHEN SMALLER STOPPERS PULL FREE

When knots that surround the standing part of a line, such as overhands and figure 8 knots, are too small, Ashley's stopper knot does the job. By bringing the working end back into play before the final tightening, a knot of satisfactory bulk is created that will be useful in sailing and other activities. Clifford W. Ashley, author of *The Ashley Book of Knots,* created this knot.

Ashley's Stopper Knot: Step 1

Tie a slipknot—a simple noose (see page 19)—in the working end.

Ashley's Stopper Knot: Step 2

Bring the working end through the back of the noose. For the best results, tighten the over-hand before bringing the working end through the loop. Then tighten the noose by pulling on the standing part to create the three overlapping strands, as shown in the photograph.

43

BOATING KNOTS: Bends

Carrick Bend

A KNOT USED FOR JOINING TWO LARGE LINES SECURELY

The carrick bend creates a very stable knot when tied correctly, even when the material in the two lines differs, such as when synthetics are joined to natural fibers. But this knot is often tied incorrectly by beginning knot tyers who weave the second working end inappropriately through the first rope's loop. The wrongly tied knot appears, on casual glance, to be a carrick bend, but it falls apart under pressure. Because of this, some knot enthusiasts refer to the knot pictured here as the *true*

Carrick Bend: Step 1	Carrick Bend: Step 2

Make a loop in the working end of the first line.	Lay the working end of the second line across the first loop, as shown in the photograph.

carrick bend. This knot has been known and often used by mariners for at least a thousand years. It appeared in print for the first time in a book of nautical terms, *Vocabulaire des Termes de Marine,* published in France in 1783. Mistakenly considered by many a strong knot, this bend actually reduces the strength of the lines by 30 percent or more.

Carrick Bend: Step 3

Bring the second working end around the back of the standing part of the first line, then over the first working end. Then bring it behind the first loop but over its own standing part where it crosses under the first loop, as shown in the photograph.

Carrick Bend: Step 4

Tighten the knot slowly by pulling on both standing parts. As the knot tightens, it will form the shape shown in the final, upper photograph. The working ends on the opposite sides of the knot create a stronger union than when the ends emerge on the same side of the knot.

Vice Versa

A KNOT USED FOR JOINING TWO LINES TOGETHER EVEN WHEN THEY ARE WET AND SLIPPERY

Slick lines, such as polyethylene or even strips of wet leather, can be joined together firmly with the vice versa. A somewhat intricate knot with quite a few crossing points, it is not terribly difficult to tie—after a few practice tyings. But beware: If the two working ends are not woven together exactly as shown, the final product will lack the security of a true vice versa, and the knot may utterly fail.

Vice Versa: Step 1

Lay the two lines alongside each other, the working ends pointing in opposite directions. Loop each line around the other, as shown in the photograph.

Vice Versa: Step 2

Bring the working end of one line through the loop in the other line (from back to front), as shown in the photograph.

Its first appearance in print seems to be from Harry Asher in *The Alternative Knot Book* (1989), but it, or something very similar, probably saw use by mariners before that. This bend may also be used by climbers.

Vice Versa: Step 3

Continue to weave the two lines together by bringing the second working end through the loop in the other line (from back to front), as shown in the photograph.

Vice Versa: Step 4

Work the knot into its distinctive shape as it is tightened, as shown in the photograph.

Zeppelin Bend

A SECURE KNOT FOR JOINING TWO LINES TOGETHER THAT CAN BE LOADED BEFORE IT IS TIGHTENED

The zeppelin bend (or Rosendahl's knot) can be loaded before the knot is tightened because it will form into its proper shape and function when loaded. This can be a great advantage should a boat being moored drift away before the knot is finished. As with many knots, there is more than one way to tie a zeppelin bend. This method is old and considered by many to be easier. This knot can also be used by campers or by anyone wishing to bend two ropes.

Zeppelin Bend: Step 1

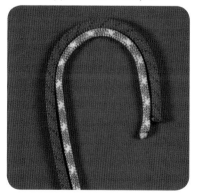

Hold the two working ends alongside each other, both pointing in the same direction, as shown in the photograph.

Zeppelin Bend: Step 2

Tie a half hitch (see page 22) in the nearest line so that it encloses the second line, as shown in the photograph.

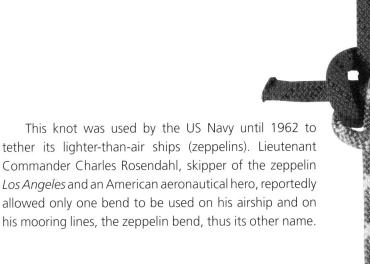

This knot was used by the US Navy until 1962 to tether its lighter-than-air ships (zeppelins). Lieutenant Commander Charles Rosendahl, skipper of the zeppelin *Los Angeles* and an American aeronautical hero, reportedly allowed only one bend to be used on his airship and on his mooring lines, the zeppelin bend, thus its other name.

Zeppelin Bend: Step 3

Bring the standing part of the second line away from the first line in the opposite direction and across the second working end, as shown in the photograph.

Zeppelin Bend: Step 4

Bring the working end of the second line through the loop in the first line and through its own loop (as shown in the photograph), forming two interlocked overhands. As soon as both standing parts are loaded, the knot will assume the proper shape and security.

Scaffold Knot

A DURABLE NOOSE (SLIDING LOOP) OFTEN USED WITH A PROTECTIVE PLASTIC OR METAL THIMBLE

More complex than the simple noose (or slipknot), yet simpler than the hangman's noose, the scaffold knot (sometimes called the gallows knot) is a sturdy loop that slides to fit snugly around a bar, rail, or other object. On boats this knot is often tightened around a thimble, a teardrop-shaped lining for the loop that protects the line from wear, creating what sailors refer to as a "hard-eye."

This is important, since the almost constant movement of boats soon wears through a line. (Thimbles are available

Scaffold Knot: Step 1

Form a loop in the working end of the line, then bring the working end around the back of the standing part.

Scaffold Knot: Step 2

Bring the working end back across the top of the loop.

in many sizes and materials—such as nylon or stainless steel—and are obtainable from suppliers who sell boating and yachting equipment.) The name suggests that this knot was used by hangmen who were less skilled in knot tying or in a rush to get the job done.

This knot can be used by campers who want a sliding loop more secure than the slipknot. It is often used by fishermen to secure a hook to the end of fishing line.

Scaffold Knot: Step 3

Bring the working end around the back of the standing part a second time, as shown in the photograph.

Scaffold Knot: Step 4

Take the working end up through both loops and tighten by pulling on the working end and the loop. Be sure the turns around the line lay down neatly against each other.

Bowline

A FIXED LOOP AT THE END OF A LINE OR FOR ATTACHING A LINE TO AN OBJECT

The bowline is one of the best known and most widely used of all knots. It creates a fixed loop that does not slip or jam. It is, however, far from being a secure knot. It can be shaken loose when unloaded, and it has been known to capsize (deform) when overloaded. It is, therefore, best backed up with a stopper (see the final photograph). But even while loaded, this knot can be untied by pushing up on the bight that surrounds the standing part. When a

Bowline: Step 1	Bowline: Step 2

Form a small loop in the standing part of the line and bring the working end back up through the loop, as shown in the photograph.	Take the working end around behind the standing part and back down through the loop. Pull slowly on the standing part to form the knot—but do not tighten the knot.

loop simply has to be untied later, the bowline is a great choice. The bowline, however, reduces the strength of a line or cord by as much as 40 percent.

Originally the bowline was used to secure a ship's square sail forward and closer to the wind. It was mentioned in *The Sea-man's Dictionary* of 1644. It is useful in jobs big and small, from securing string before tying a package to securing a gear bag to be hauled up a cliff by climbers. The size of the loop, from very small to very large, is determined by the tyer. More trustworthy variations of the bowline, such as the double bowline (see page 56) and the triple bowline (see page 58), are also covered in this book.

Bowline: Step 3

Adjust the main loop to the required size, and tighten the knot.

Bowline: Step 4

Finish with an overhand stopper (see page 6) to add security to the bowline.

Bowline on a Bight

A FIXED DOUBLE LOOP THAT CAN BE
TIED IN THE MIDDLE OF A LINE

Bowline on a bight, bowline in the bight, bowline upon the bight—they are all names for the same knot. This knot can be tied near a working end of a rope but more often appears away from an end. Historically, this knot served as an improvised seat, the seated person shoving one leg through one loop, the other leg through the other loop. The person in the seat held on to the line and was then lowered or raised, as over the side of a ship. When a double loop is tied in the middle of a rope, a weight (such as a person) can be lowered or raised from two points, allowing

Bowline on a Bight: Step 1

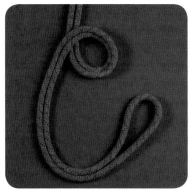

With the line doubled, form a loop in the doubled line as if a basic bowline (see page 52) was being tied.

Bowline on a Bight: Step 2

Take the double end up through the loop, again as if a basic bowline was being tied.

for more security and control during the process. Because devices such as harnesses now exist to aid in moving a person via a rope, the bowline on a bight is not recommended for such use except in emergencies. This knot first appeared in print in 1795 in *Allgemeines Wörterbuch der Marine* by Johann Röding. It is often used by campers and climbers who need to secure gear to the middle of a rope. *Note:* The bowline on a bight reduces the strength of the line by as much as 40 percent.

Bowline on a Bight: Step 3

Take the end of the single loop down and around the end of the double loop.

Bowline on a Bight: Step 4

Continue to bring the end of the single loop over the knot that has now been created in the line. Adjust the size of the double loop to the desired dimension before tightening.

Double Bowline

A VARIATION OF THE BASIC BOWLINE THAT ADDS SECURITY TO THE KNOT

A second loop at the beginning of a double bowline doubles the pressure on the working end and provides greater security. The finished knot does *not* have two loops, even though the name implies that it might. If a double loop is needed, use the bowline on a bight (see page 54). This knot reduces the strength of a line by only 25 to 30 percent, making it an overall stronger knot than

Double Bowline: Step 1	Double Bowline: Step 2

Form a loop in the working end of the rope as if a basic bowline (see page 52) was being tied.	Form a second loop, a duplicate of the first loop, and lay it on top of the first loop.

the basic bowline or the bowline on a bight. A stopper knot in the working end also adds security. You may see this knot, as with other variations of the bowline, being used by campers and climbers.

Double Bowline: Step 3

Bring the working end up through both loops and in back of the standing part as if tying a basic bowline.

Double Bowline: Step 4

Bring the working end down through both loops and tighten the knot. As with the basic bowline, a stopper knot in the working end adds even more security.

Triple Bowline

A FIXED TRIPLE LOOP THAT CREATES A MORE SECURE EMERGENCY "CHAIR"

The triple bowline is no more than a basic bowline tied on a long bight in a manner that creates three loops. Since it is tied on a bight, it can be tied in the middle of a rope if needed. With a fair amount of painstaking effort, the size of each loop can be adjusted to differing sizes. This allows the knot to be used as a chair (with each of two loops around someone's legs and the third loop around the torso under the arms). As with other knots used as chairs, the triple bowline is recommended

Triple Bowline: Step 1	Triple Bowline: Step 2

Make a long bight in the rope and form a loop as if beginning to tie a basic bowline (see page 52).	Take the doubled end up through the loop and around, behind the standing part.

only when no other means of raising or lowering a person is available. This knot sees very little use today, but it is highly useful when it is needed. Its origin remains somewhat in doubt. It may have been developed by climbers, not sailors, to anchor one rope to three different points.

Triple Bowline: Step 3

Take the doubled end back down through the loop. (At this point, you are on your way to tying a bowline on a bight.)

Triple Bowline: Step 4

The doubled end becomes the third of three loops in the finished knot. Adjust the size of the loops, and tighten the knot.

59

Midshipman's Hitch

A SLIDE-AND-GRIP LOOP FOR SUSPENDING OBJECTS OR ADDING TENSION TO A LINE

The midshipman's hitch is another misnamed knot. Not actually a hitch at all, the knot is a slide-and-grip *loop* that can be adjusted when something needs to be suspended at a specific height or a line needs to have slack taken out. When a load is applied to this knot, it deforms the standing part of the line at enough of an angle to cause the knot to grip firmly. When the load is off, the knot slides freely. If the working end is left long enough, a stopper knot can be tied around the standing part of the line, giving this knot a semipermanent

Midshipman's Hitch: Step 1

Form a loop in the working end of the rope.

Midshipman's Hitch: Step 2

Take the working end around the standing part and up through the loop.

position on the line. This knot may be used by campers to add tension to tent lines and by climbers to hang gear.

There was no officer more junior in the British Royal Navy than one with the rank of midshipman. The name of midshipman's hitch suggests a knot of naval birth that performs less than perfectly. The knot, however, deserves a high rating in utility.

Midshipman's Hitch: Step 3	Midshipman's Hitch: Step 4

Take the working end around the standing part and up through the loop a second time, taking care to make the second turn overlap the first turn as shown in the photograph.	With the working end, tie a half hitch (see page 22) around the standing part above the loop. The knot can be moved to adjust the size of the loop. When it is tightened and the loop loaded, the knot will grip.

61

BOATING KNOTS: Hitches

Anchor (Fisherman's) Bend

A RELATIVELY STRONG AND SECURE HITCH, ESPECIALLY FOR WET OR SLICK LINES

The anchor bend (also known as the fisherman's bend) is another misnamed knot. It is actually a useful *hitch,* handy for such jobs as securing the mooring lines of small crafts to mooring rings. It's on the strong side, reducing the strength of a line by only 25 to 30 percent, and it works well in lines slippery from wetness or the slickness of the material, such as polypropylene. The anchor bend

<table>
<tr><td>

Anchor (Fisherman's) Bend: Step 1

Take the working end of the line over or through the anchoring point.

</td><td>

Anchor (Fisherman's) Bend: Step 2

Take the working end around or through the anchoring point a second time.

</td></tr>
</table>

is a variation of the round turn and two half hitches (see page 86). This knot may also be used by campers to, for instance, suspend a bag from the limb of a tree.

Anchor (Fisherman's) Bend: Step 3

Bring the working end across the standing part and through both turns in the line that is around or through the anchoring point. You have now tied a half hitch through two loops.

Anchor (Fisherman's) Bend: Step 4

Snug up the first half hitch and tie a second half hitch around the standing part. Tighten the entire knot.

Buntline Hitch

A VERY SECURE KNOT FOR CONDITIONS WHERE THE LINE AND ATTACHMENT POINT WILL BE SHAKEN VIGOROUSLY

The buntline hitch would be more accurately named a noose, since it slides on the line after being tied, but it is used for jobs that require a hitch. It could be described as a clove hitch (see page 24) with the working end tied around the standing part. On sailing ships the buntline was attached to the bottom of sails so they could be drawn up to spill the wind. The hitch, therefore, needed

Buntline Hitch: Step 1	Buntline Hitch: Step 2
	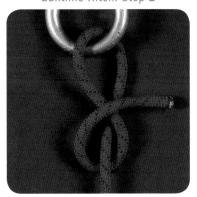
Take the working end of the rope through or around the attachment point and back across the standing part to form a loop.	**Bring the working end fully around the standing part.**

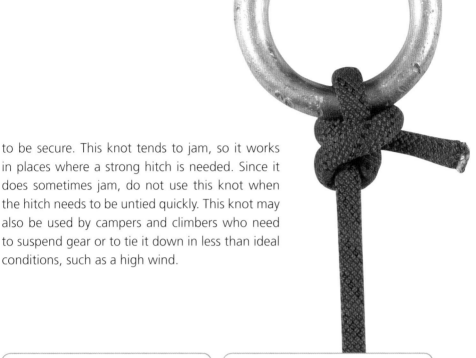

to be secure. This knot tends to jam, so it works in places where a strong hitch is needed. Since it does sometimes jam, do not use this knot when the hitch needs to be untied quickly. This knot may also be used by campers and climbers who need to suspend gear or to tie it down in less than ideal conditions, such as a high wind.

Buntline Hitch: Step 3

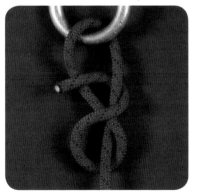

Take the working end around and through the loop from the back, as shown in the photograph.

Buntline Hitch: Step 4

Tuck the working end back through the knot, forming a half hitch. The final tuck of the working end within the knot makes the buntline hitch work. Tighten the knot, then pull the standing part to snug the knot against the attachment point.

Highwayman's Hitch

A HITCH FOR SITUATIONS WHERE A QUICK RELEASE MIGHT BE NEEDED

When a temporary hitch is needed, such as when mooring a small craft for a short amount of time, the highwayman's hitch (also known as a draw hitch) does an excellent job. It works well for lowering light loads, like lowering a gear bag over the side of a tall ship. Whether or not it was used by highwaymen (robbers) as a quick-release tether for horses, when a fast getaway was part of the job, is not known, but it works well for temporarily tethering animals.

Highwayman's Hitch: Step 1

Form a loop in the working end of the rope and hold it behind the attachment point. A long working end will be needed to complete this knot.

Highwayman's Hitch: Step 2

Form a second loop in the working end and hold it over the front of the attachment point.

As a bonus, it can be tied in the middle of a line and released from a distance. This knot may also be used by campers, but do not use this knot for heavy work, since it can fall apart earlier than required.

Pass the second loop through the first loop.

Form a third loop in the working end of the rope, and take this in front of the attachment point and through the second loop, leaving enough of a tail on the working end to easily grab. Tighten by holding the third loop in place while pulling on the standing part. With a quick tug on the working end, the knot falls completely apart.

Camel Hitch

A HITCH FOR SITUATIONS WHERE THE LOAD MIGHT BE APPLIED IN ANY DIRECTION FROM THE KNOT

The camel hitch makes an excellent knot choice when the load applied to the hitch might shift from one direction to another. It works well on cylindrical and flat objects, and it can be used to attach a smaller line to a larger one. Whether wet or dry, it comes undone easily. And, yes, it would work to tether a camel—or any other animal. This knot is used in camping, for example, when attaching a tent line to a stake via a secure hitch.

Camel Hitch: Step 1	Camel Hitch: Step 2

Camel Hitch: Step 1

With the working end, make two full turns around the bar, rail, or other attachment point.

Camel Hitch: Step 2

Take the working end across the front of the standing part, around the attachment point, and down through itself twice, as shown in the photograph. Work the completed hitch tight by pulling on the working end and standing part simultaneously. For greater security, make the last two turns into two half hitches (see page 23), one tight against the other.

Rolling Hitch

A HITCH FOR SITUATIONS WHERE THE LOAD WILL BE APPLIED AT AN ANGLE TO THE KNOT OTHER THAN A RIGHT ANGLE

Many hitches suffer a loss of security when the load is applied in a direction other than a right angle. The rolling hitch does not suffer such a loss as long as the tension is relatively steady. It is, in effect, another modification of the clove hitch (see page 24). It works well on any cylindrical object, including the tying of a smaller line to a larger one.

Rolling Hitch: Step 1

With the working end, make two turns around the object or around the larger line.

Rolling Hitch: Step 2

Take the working end back up over the standing part. Make another turn around the object or larger line from underneath, and bring the working end out underneath itself (as shown in the photograph). Tighten the turns by pulling on the working end and the standing part simultaneously. When the load is applied, the knot grips the object or line.

Pole Hitch

THIS KNOT GATHERS AND BINDS TOGETHER ASSORTED LONG OBJECTS

Poles, paddles, oars, and any long objects (including long-handled tools such as brooms and rakes) are gathered closely together and bound with the pole hitch. To prevent creating an awkward armload, use two of these knots, one toward each end of the long objects.

The pole hitch not only works for ease of carrying but also for storing long objects. Note that

Pole Hitch: Step 1

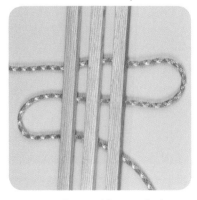

Arrange the cord beneath the long objects in an S or Z shape.

Pole Hitch: Step 2

Bring the ends of the rope over the objects and through the opposite bights, as shown in the photograph.

the pole hitch is actually a combination of a hitch with a final securing knot to complete the binding. This knot is easier to manage when the length of rope or cord being used is just long enough to do the job.

Pole Hitch: Step 3

Draw the objects together, bringing both ends of the rope to the same side of the objects, as shown in the photograph.

Pole Hitch: Step 4

Secure the ends with a square (reef) knot (see page 13).

Pile (Post) Hitch

A QUICK, SIMPLE, AND SECURE ATTACHMENT TO PILE, POST, OR STAKE

For fast mooring of a craft to a pile, use the pile hitch. By tying the knot midline, tension can be pulled in two directions from the knot, making this great for putting up a barrier rope between a series of uprights. It has numerous other uses, such as tying a tent line to a stake. It unties with extreme ease.

Pile (Post) Hitch: Step 1	Pile (Post) Hitch: Step 2

Double the section of line to be attached and wrap it around the pile or post.	Take the loop over the top of the pile or post, then pull on the standing part to tighten. *Note:* The knot can be pushed down the pile or post before being tightened.

Constrictor Knot

A BINDING KNOT THAT SIMPLY DOES NOT COME UNDONE

This variation on the clove hitch (see page 24), once loaded or otherwise fully tightened, refuses to come undone. When fully tightened, it is often easier to cut off than untie. When used as a semipermanent binding, the rope or cord can be trimmed off short on both sides of the knot.

Constrictor Knot: Step 1	Constrictor Knot: Step 2

With the working end of the line, tie a clove hitch (see page 24) around the attachment point.	Tuck the working end under the first turn of the clove hitch and tighten. *Note:* When the knot will need to be untied, the final tuck can be made as a draw loop (see page 7).

73

Double Constrictor Knot

A VARIATION OF THE CONSTRICTOR KNOT
THAT BINDS EVEN MORE SECURELY

When ultimate power in a binding knot is required, the double constrictor, the best of all binding knots, is the answer. It has been compared to the grip of a boa constrictor. When the diameter of whatever this knot is tied to is large, the basic constrictor knot (see page 73) loses some of its strength— and thus the double constrictor would come into play. It can be used, for example, as a substitute for hose clamps. With a short length of cord, the double constrictor knot works great to hold a sack without a drawstring closed.

Double Constrictor Knot: Step 1

Take the working end of the line around the object and across itself.

Double Constrictor Knot: Step 2

Take the working end around the object a second time and across itself a second time, maintaining the diagonal direction as shown in the photograph.

This knot works extremely well for attaching cords to the handles of tools, or anything else of similar design, to allow them to be hung. It can be used to attach a pencil to a clipboard.

The final tuck in tying the double constrictor can be made as a quick-release draw loop if you want to untie the knot later. For the very best results, use a hard rope or cord when tying the knot to soft material, such as a soft line, and use a soft rope or cord when tying the knot to hard material, such a metal ring.

Double Constrictor Knot: Step 3

Bring the working end over the standing part and tuck it under the pair of diagonal turns as shown in the photograph.

Double Constrictor Knot: Step 4

Tuck the working end under the remaining single turn and tighten by working all the slack out of the knot.

Munter-Mule hitch with Figure 8 backup

Prusik, Blake Hitch, Double Figure 8, Figure 8

Bachmann Hitch

A FRICTION KNOT FOR ASCENDING A ROPE WITH A CARABINER

The Bachmann hitch attaches a carabiner to a rope with strong cord or webbing so that the carabiner can be used as a handle. Without a load, the hitch slides freely up the rope. Once weight is applied, the hitch grips the rope, preventing the load from slipping back down the rope. The greater the difference between the diameter of the cord of the hitch and the diameter of the main rope, the greater the grip of the hitch. This knot could be used to

Bachmann Hitch: Step 1	Bachmann Hitch: Step 2

Attach a carabiner to a loop and place the loop around the rope, as shown in the photograph. (You can tie a loop with the double fisherman's knot on page 90.)	Bring the end of the loop around the rope and through the carabiner.

hang a load from a vertically suspended rope, such as hanging a food bag while camping, in which case the weight should be attached to the loop or sling, not to the carabiner, to prevent slipping.

Bachmann Hitch: Step 3

Bring the end of the loop around the rope and through the carabiner a second time.

Bachmann Hitch: Step 4

Bring the end of the loop around the rope and through the carabiner a third time. If the hitch does not grip adequately, you may add another turn of the loop. The knot must finish with the loop pulled out through the carabiner.

Munter (Italian) Hitch

USED FOR IMPROVISING A BELAY OR A RAPPEL DEVICE WITH THE USE OF ONE OR TWO CARABINERS

The Munter hitch works as a climbing device for belaying and rappelling and should be learned by all climbers. The knot grips a carabiner when a load is applied, but the rope runs through the carabiner when the load is off. It should be used with one locking carabiner or two non-locking carabiners with the gates reversed. Test the knot on safe ground by pulling aggressively on the standing part before trusting it to save a life! Werner Munter, a Swiss guide, popularized this knot, leaving his name in the annals of climbing.

Munter Hitch: Step 1

Twist a coil into the rope with the upper and lower strands of the coil folded together, as shown in the photograph.

Munter Hitch: Step 2

Clip the carabiner into both sides of the folded strands with the spine of the carabiner next to the strand that will bear the load.

Girth Hitch

USED FOR QUICKLY ATTACHING A LOOP TO ANY OBJECT

Simple and fast to apply, the girth hitch (or ring hitch) has many uses. It attaches a pre-sewn or pre-tied loop or sling to any fixed object. It can be used to connect loops or attach a loop to a climbing harness from which gear can be hung. Climbers often use a girth hitch in slings of webbing, but it works in any type of rope or cordage. This knot is often used in camping and could be helpful to boaters for numerous jobs, such as creating loops from which gear can be hung.

Girth Hitch: Step 1

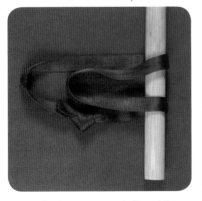

Pass the loop around the object to which it is to be attached. (The loop in the photograph is tied with a water knot from page 92.)

Girth Hitch: Step 2

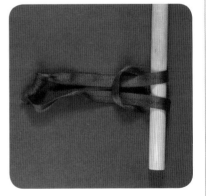

Bring one half of the loop through the other half and tighten by pulling on the lower half. As you tighten the hitch, work the knot that ties the webbing or cord into a loop to the side of the loop, not at the bottom where it could get in the way.

Klemheist Knot

A FRICTION KNOT FOR ASCENDING A ROPE OR ESCAPING A BELAY

When tied properly, the klemheist knot (or Machard knot) grips the rope when weighted but releases and slides along the rope when the load is off. It releases and slides with more ease than the prusik knot (see page 84) but grips with less tenacity than the prusik. It works well for tying off a climber's rope to allow escape from the belay.

Klemheist Knot: Step 1	Klemheist Knot: Step 2

Wrap a loop of cord or a sling of webbing four or five times around the rope and toward the load, keeping the wraps neatly laid against the rope.	Pass the lower end of the loop through the upper end and clip a carabiner into the lower loop. (You can add more wraps if the knot slips.)

Garda Knot

A RATCHETING KNOT THAT EMPLOYS TWO CARABINERS AND IS USEFUL IN HAULING

The Garda knot ratchets, allowing the rope to pass through a pair of carabiners in one direction only. The two carabiners should be the same size and shape, and they should not be locking carabiners, since the locks prevent them from pinching the rope firmly enough for the knot to work. This knot might also be useful in camping. *Note:* If the rope rides up onto the gates when the knot is in use, the Garda may come unclipped. This can be prevented by maintaining tension on the rope.

Garda Knot: Step 1	Garda Knot: Step 2
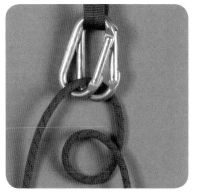	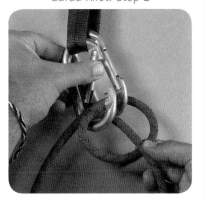
Clip two carabiners into a sling, side by side, with the gates facing in the same direction. Pass the rope through both carabiners and form a loop, as shown in the photograph.	Pass the loop through the first carabiner only. Slide the loop onto the spines of the carabiners, the sides opposite to the gates, before loading the system.

83

Prusik Knot

A FRICTION KNOT USED FOR ASCENDING A ROPE

As with the klemheist knot (see page 82), the prusik slides up the rope when unloaded but grips the rope firmly when loaded, so it is actually a slide-and-grip hitch. A big difference, however, is in the fact that the prusik grips the rope better, so much so that it may be difficult to break free after being loaded with a heavy weight. But it can be broken free by loosening the "tongue" (center loop) first. This knot is a better choice for new, wet, or otherwise slippery rope.

Credited to Dr. Karl Prusik, circa 1931, the prusik knot can be tied with one hand, a useful skill in an emergency when the other hand may be unavailable. The word "prusik" may be used to refer not only to the knot but also to the loop of cord in which the knot is tied and

Prusik Knot: Step 1	Prusik Knot: Step 2

Tie a loop in a cord of significantly smaller diameter than the main rope.	Attach the loop to the main rope with a girth hitch (see page 81), keeping the hitch loose.

to the ascending technique: "to prusik." Many climbers today utilize mechanical ascenders instead of the prusik knot. Mechanical ascenders damage a rope more than the prusik, but the prusik will fail (slip) if it is overloaded, a problem rarely seen with mechanical devices. This knot might be used in camping for such tasks as hanging bags on ropes suspended vertically to keep the bags out of animal reach.

Prusik Knot: Step 3

Bring the loop around the rope and back through the hitch a second time.

Prusik Knot: Step 4

Bring the loop around and through a third time. Lay the wraps of loop evenly and without twists to maximize the bite on the rope. Tighten the knot against the rope. Test the knot, and if it slips, add more wraps.

Round Turn and Two Half Hitches

A VARIATION OF TWO HALF HITCHES THAT CREATES A KNOT OF UNPARALLELED STRENGTH

Not only strong and dependable, this knot, when tied correctly, never jams. Because weight applied to the standing part pulls the rope in a straight line, the breaking strength is not diminished by the round turn and two half hitches. It is useful for securing one end of a rope when the other end will be used to fasten down bulky objects. You will find this knot useful in camping and boating as well as climbing.

Round Turn & Two Half Hitches:
Step 1

Take the working end of the rope around an object in a full round turn.

Round Turn & Two Half Hitches:
Step 2

Tie two half hitches (see page 23) in the working end. Remember to tighten the first half hitch before tying the second.

CLIMBING KNOTS: Bends

Hunter's (Rigger's) Bend

USED FOR JOINING TWO ROPES IN A TIGHT, STRONG, AND SECURE-WHEN-LOADED KNOT

Based on the interweaving of two overhand knots, the hunter's bend is quickly and easily learned. It tightens securely when loaded, but it can be worked loose and separated when the load is off. This bend is well worth knowing any time the joining of two ropes is needed and is useful in activities other than climbing.

Hunter's (Rigger's) Bend: Step 1	Hunter's (Rigger's) Bend: Step 2

Tie an overhand knot at the working end of the first rope, but do not tighten it.	Thread the working end of the second rope through the loop of the overhand knot in the first rope. Bring the end of the second rope around and back through the loop of the first overhand a second time, forming an overhand knot in the second rope, as shown in the photograph. Tighten.

Fisherman's Knot

A SIMPLE, QUICK-TYING KNOT FOR JOINING TWO ROPES OF SIMILAR DIAMETER

One of the most common bends used by climbers, the compact fisherman's knot combines two overhand knots that jam against each other when pressure is applied. Simple to tie even with cold, wet hands, this knot has earned its popularity—and it works well in the stiffest cordage. It unties fairly easily, even after being weighted, but it can bind up after being shock-loaded. The knot works best in ropes of similar thickness and, therefore,

Fisherman's Knot: Step 1	Fisherman's Knot: Step 2
	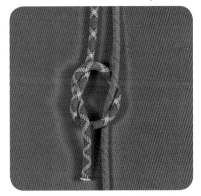
Form an overhand knot at the working end of the first rope.	**Thread the working end of the second rope through the overhand knot in the first rope, as shown in the photograph.**

does a fine job of tying two ends of the same rope or cord together.

Since it works very well in lines of very small diameter, such as fishing line, it is popular with anglers, so much so that the knot bears their name. But fishermen called this knot the water knot in the 1600s and 1700s, later referring to it as the angler's knot. It has also been called the English knot, the Englishman's knot, the waterman's knot, and the true lover's knot.

Fisherman's Knot: Step 3

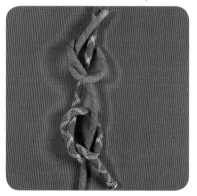

Tie an overhand knot in the working end of the second rope. The second overhand must be tied around the first rope, as shown in the photograph.

Fisherman's Knot: Step 4

Tighten both overhand knots and draw them together slowly by pulling on the standing parts of both ropes.

Double Fisherman's Knot

ONE OF THE SAFEST, MOST SECURE KNOTS FOR JOINING TWO ROPES OF SIMILAR DIAMETER

As the name implies, the double fisherman's knot extends the fisherman's knot (see page 88), joining two ropes or lines of similar size in an extremely secure knot. In the double fisherman's, two double overhand knots jam against each other when pressure is applied. It is an excellent choice when using synthetic cordage, including fishing line. It works in natural fiber cordage, of course, but it can become extremely difficult to untie from anything other than synthetics.

Double Fisherman's Knot: Step 1	Double Fisherman's Knot: Step 2

Tie a double overhand knot (see page 42) at the working end of the first rope.	Thread the working end of the second rope through both loops of the double overhand knot in the first rope, as shown in the photograph.

After being weighted the two double overhands form a tight bond that simply stays put. For this reason, climbers will use this knot to create a short sling or loop to aid climbing. Fishermen often call the double fisherman's knot the grinner knot for reasons not completely understood. Perhaps it's because it looks to some like open mouths prior to being tightened.

Double Fisherman's Knot: Step 3

Tighten the double overhand in the first rope.

Double Fisherman's Knot: Step 4

At this point it will be easier to continue if you reverse the knot assembly in your hand.

Tie a double overhand in the working end of the second rope, making sure both loops of the knot are around the standing part of the first rope. Tighten the second double overhand and draw both knots together slowly by pulling on the standing part of both ropes.

Water Knot

JOINS TWO ENDS OF A LENGTH OF TUBULAR NYLON WEBBING INTO A LOOP OR TWO LENGTHS OF WEBBING

Most climbers today use webbing sewn into slings (or runners) by a manufacturer. Webbing is nylon woven stoutly into a tubular shape, then flattened. If, however, you need to tie a sling or loop, or tie two lengths of webbing together, the relatively simple water knot works well. It is created by weaving two overhand knots together, one the mirror image of the other. It can be tied in any material, including rope and fishing line. Although this knot creates a very secure bend in cord, twine, and monofilaments, it almost always tightens irretrievably in small lines. Water knots in

Water Knot: Step 1	Water Knot: Step 2

Form an overhand knot in the end of the webbing, making sure the webbing is arranged to allow the knot to lie flat if pressed.	Slide the second end of webbing into the first overhand knot, as if you're tracing the knot. Start at the point where the first end of webbing leaves the first overhand knot, as shown in the photograph.

webbing may have a tendency to creep apart and should be used in climbing with at least 3 inches of tail on both ends and/or with the tails fixed with adhesive tape.

Webbing is known as tape to some, and this knot is called by those same people the tape knot. *Hutton's Dictionary,* published in 1815, referred to this knot as the ring knot, and it may also be known as the ring bend. Older publications call it the gut knot, an indication that it has been around a long time, certainly long before synthetic lines.

Water Knot: Step 3	Water Knot: Step 4

Continue to follow the lead of the first piece of webbing through the overhand knot with the second end of webbing, making sure both ends of webbing lie flat against each other.	When both ends of webbing have been woven into one overhand knot, tighten it by pulling on the working ends of the webbing. Before trusting the knot to stop a fall, load it with body weight to set it as tight as possible.

Figure 8 Bend

A MORE COMPLEX KNOT USED FOR SECURELY JOINING TWO ROPES OF SIMILAR SIZE AND CONSTRUCTION

The figure 8 bend is created by weaving together two figure 8 knots. Climbers tend to prefer this bend because of its security as well as the strength of the interwoven working ends. If heavily loaded, this knot may prove impossible to untie if the ropes are of approximately the same diameter. It does hold nearly as well in ropes of dissimilar diameter. Despite its security, climbers often leave the working ends long enough to back up the knot with stoppers, adding

Figure 8 Bend: Step 1	Figure 8 Bend: Step 2

Tie a figure 8 knot (see page 10) in the working end of one rope.	Thread the working end of the second rope into the figure 8 knot in the first rope, as shown in the photograph.

even more security (not a bad idea when your life may depend on your knot).

Clifford Ashley, arguably the greatest knot-man of all times, called the figure 8 bend a Flemish bend and found it, reportedly, a bothersome knot to deal with. This knot may also be used by campers and boaters.

Figure 8 Bend: Step 3

Continue to follow the lead of the first rope. The goal is to create a second figure 8 knot that duplicates but is a mirror image of the first figure 8 knot.

Figure 8 Bend: Step 4

When both ropes have been woven into one figure 8 knot, carefully compress and tighten the composite knot into the characteristic figure 8 shape. For the greatest strength, make sure the standing part of both ropes forms the outer bight at both ends of the knot.

Figure 8 Follow-Through

A FIXED LOOP,
THE STANDARD TIE-IN KNOT FOR CLIMBERS

Since the tie-in knot is where a climber is attached to a climbing rope, it is of critical importance, since the climber could fall and depend on the rope—and the knot—for life. The figure 8 follow-through is most often chosen. If you can know only one knot well, beginning climbers are often told, the figure 8 follow-through is the one.

It is not only a strong and secure loop but easy to visually inspect for correctness. The working end follows the path of the rope through a figure 8 that has already been tied, thus the name. The figure 8 follow-through is no more than a figure 8 loop (see page 16), but it is tied differently—in this case the loop being often

Figure 8 Follow-Through: Step 1	Figure 8 Follow-Through: Step 2

Tie a figure 8 knot (see page 10) in the working end of the rope. You will need this knot to be 2 to 3 feet from the end of the rope.	With the working end, begin to trace, or follow the lead of, the first figure 8, as shown in the photograph.

tied around an object, most often the climber's harness. Sometimes called the Flemish bend, it is not a bend—the Flemish bend is another name for the figure 8 bend, a knot used for tying two different ropes together. Before trusting this knot to save your life, leave enough working end to back up the knot with a stopper. The double overhand (see page 42) is an excellent choice. The figure 8 follow-through may also be used by campers and boaters, typically in situations where someone's life is *not* on the line.

Figure 8 Follow-Through: Step 3

Continue to follow the lead of the figure 8.

Figure 8 Follow-Through: Step 4

The working end needs to come out of the knot in line with the standing part, as shown in the photograph.

Figure 8 Double Loop

A VARIATION OF THE FIGURE 8 THAT CREATES TWIN LOOPS IN THE ROPE

The figure 8 double loop (sometimes called "bunny ears") creates twin loops that allow a climber to secure one rope to two anchors. Once mastered, this knot ties quickly and forms two secure fixed loops that will not alter in size when weight is applied to either or both loops. If loops of differing sizes are needed, however, the loops can be adjusted to different sizes during the tying—and they too will remain secure.

As with the double bowline (see page 56), the figure 8 double loop could be used in an emergency as a chair

Figure 8 Double Loop: Step 1	Figure 8 Double Loop: Step 2
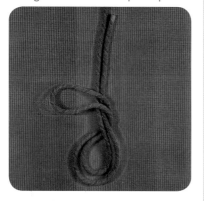	
Form a large bight in the rope and twist the bight into a loop as if starting a simple figure 8 (see page 10).	Reach through the loop and grasp the doubled rope, as shown in the photograph.

sling to raise or lower a person if, of course, the loops are made large enough. When used as a chair sling, both these knots share the common characteristic of being highly uncomfortable. This knot was first described in print in 1944 by Clifford Ashley. How long it was in use prior to Ashley's description is not known.

Figure 8 Double Loop: Step 3

Bring the doubled rope through the loop as if tying a figure 8 with draw loop (see page 12). The doubled section of rope pulled through the loop will become the double loop.

Figure 8 Double Loop: Step 4

Bring the remaining single loop down in front of the knot, take the doubled loops through the single loop, and move the single loop up to the top of the knot. Carefully tighten every-thing.

Figure 8 Triple Loop

A VARIATION OF THE FIGURE 8 THAT CREATES THREE LOOPS IN THE ROPE

The figure 8 triple loop (sometimes called the triple figure 8 loop) creates three loops that allow a climber to secure one rope to three anchors. Once mastered, this knot ties quickly and forms three secure fixed loops that will not alter in size once the final knot is tightened. As with the triple bowline (see page 58), the figure 8 triple loop could be used, in an emergency, as a chair sling to raise or lower

Figure 8 Triple Loop: Step 1

Form a large bight in the rope and twist the bight into a loop as if starting a simple figure 8 (see page 10).

Figure 8 Triple Loop: Step 2

Reach through the loop and grasp the doubled rope. Bring the doubled rope through the loop as if tying a figure 8 with draw loop (see page 12). You are now at a point where you could tie a figure 8 double loop (see page 98).

a person, with one loop for each leg and the third loop around the torso beneath the armpits. Though not recommended except in extreme circumstances, it could be used to lower an unconscious person. This knot could also be used by campers and boaters who want to attach three objects to the end of one rope.

Figure 8 Triple Loop: Step 3	Figure 8 Triple Loop: Step 4

Bring the remaining single loop over the top of the knot.	Bring this loop down through the original loop to create three loops. Carefully tighten everything. (The three loops in the photograph are smaller than most climbers would need but are shown small for photo-graphic purposes.)

Loop Knot

THE QUICKEST AND SIMPLEST LOOP IN THE MIDDLE OF A ROPE, AND FOR EMERGENCY "REPAIR" OF A DAMAGED ROPE

When something needs to be attached midrope, the loop knot works well. This knot is important for shortening and keeping a damaged rope functional. With the damaged part in the middle of the knot, at the top of the bight, it is put under no strain. Using a knot to "strengthen" a damaged rope is an emergency measure to prevent the rope from failing before the climb has ended. Be warned: Any damaged climbing rope needs to be replaced as soon as possible. And also be warned: The loop knot is not designed to bear critical weight. For a critical weight-bearing midrope knot, use the alpine butterfly (see page 103).

Loop Knot: Step 1

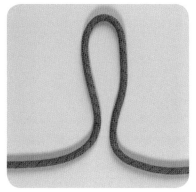

Form a bight in the rope.

Loop Knot: Step 2

Tie an overhand knot (see page 6) in the bight. Tighten by pulling slowly on the loop and the main sections of the rope.

102

Alpine Butterfly

FORMS A FIXED LOOP IN THE STANDING PART OF A ROPE

This knot with the loveliest of names creates a fixed loop at any point in a rope, a loop to which anything may be clipped or otherwise attached. It is often used in climbing as a knot to which a climber may be attached to the rope. It is especially popular in glacier travel, where it is common to find three climbers attached to one rope, one climber at each end and one in the middle.

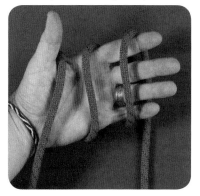

Alpine Butterfly: Step 1

Wrap the rope around your left hand twice, as shown in the photograph.

Alpine Butterfly: Step 2

Move the turn closest to your fingertips to lie between the other two turns.

Unlike the loop knot (see page 102), the alpine butterfly can and safely does serve to bear a critical load. It stands up to tension from either direction without weakening.

In addition to strength and security, the alpine butterfly almost always unties easily, even after being heavily loaded, something other loops fail to do. As with other loops, this knot can be used to isolate—within the loop of the knot—a worn or otherwise

Alpine Butterfly: Step 3

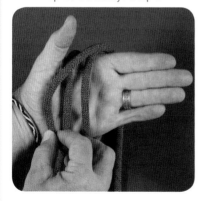

Move the turn that is now closest to your fingertips to lie closest to your thumb.

Alpine Butterfly: Step 4

Bring the turn now closest to your thumb underneath the other two turns toward your fingertips. By grasping the loop, you can now remove the rope from your hand.

weakened point of a rope. And it may be used in camping, boating, or any time an object needs to be attached to a rope at a point other than the end.

As with so many members of the knot world, this one can be tied in several different ways. This way is relatively easy to visualize.

Alpine Butterfly: Step 5

Shape the knot by pulling on the loop and the two main sections of the rope.

Alpine Butterfly: Step 6

Tighten the knot by pulling on the two main sections of the rope.

105

Spanish Bowline

TWO SEPARATE AND INDEPENDENT FIXED LOOPS USEFUL IN MOUNTAIN RESCUE WORK

The Spanish bowline, also known as the chair knot, is a very strong knot. It is safe and holds securely even under a great load. It can be used to hoist large, heavy objects, such as equipment. In rescue work one loop goes over a person's head and down under the armpits, the other loop around the legs behind the knees, allowing an unconscious person to be lowered down a mountainside (or over the side of a

Spanish Bowline: Step 1

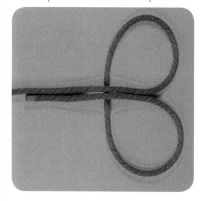

Form two loops in the working end of the rope, as shown in the photograph.

Spanish Bowline: Step 2

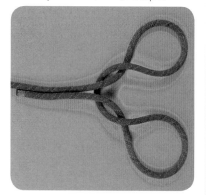

Twist each loop separately toward the center of the knot.

large ship and into a boat below). For use with a conscious person, one loop goes around each leg and the person being lowered holds on to the rope. The loops are easy to adjust during tying, since the rope moves freely through the knot.

On the downside, the ease of adjustment of the loops means the final knot must be set very tight before use or the loops could alter in size when the knot is weighted. Since better methods of attaching people to ropes have been developed, such as pre-sewn chairs, it

Spanish Bowline: Step 3

Reach through the right-hand loop and grasp the left-hand loop.

Spanish Bowline: Step 4

Bring the left loop through the right loop.

is not recommended to use the Spanish bowline as a chair except in emergencies. Knotmaster Clifford Ashley referred to this knot by the unwieldy name of a double splayed loop in the bight.

Spanish Bowline: Step 5	Spanish Bowline: Step 6

Reach through both loops simultaneously (using both hands) and grasp the points of the newly formed lower loop at the top, where indicated in the photograph.	Bring the two points indicated out through the upper loops to form two new loops. Painstakingly adjust the final loops to the required size, and pull strongly on the central knot to tighten. (These loops are smaller than most climbers would need but are shown small for photographic purposes.) Have patience when adjusting the final loops, as this will take practice.

Interlocking Loops

A KNOT USED TO JOIN TWO PIECES OF CORDAGE WITH LOOPS TIED IN THE WORKING ENDS

Interlocking loops can be tied in any material of any size. (As an example, fly-fishing line is shown in the photographs.) They remove the strain on the actual knots that form the loops and create a strong connection between two ropes, lines, or cords. The loops must be interlocked correctly or one line will cut through the other. The loops must interlock to form a square knot (see page 13), *not* a girth hitch (see page 81).

Interlocking Loops: Step 1

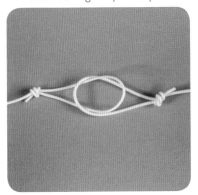

Tie a loop in the working end of both lines. (Many knots will work to create the loops. An overhand on a bight is used in the photographs.) Lay one loop inside the other, as shown in the photograph.

Interlocking Loops: Step 2

Bring the knot of the outer loop, and the rest of that line, through the inner loop.

Monkey's Fist.

Overhand Knot being used as a stopper.

MISCELLANEOUS KNOTS

Sheepshank

A KNOT FOR
SHORTENING ANY LINE
TO ANY REQUIRED LENGTH

The sheepshank allows a line to be shortened to a required length without cutting. It can also be tied with a damaged section of line in the middle of the knot to take strain off the damaged section. It ties and unties easily and holds well under tension. But if the sheepshank is to be loaded, it must be done slowly and cautiously, since it can fall apart easily. So fully tighten the knot and apply the load (the tension) gradually rather than suddenly. Two half hitches may be tied at each end instead of one for more security.

Sheepshank: Step 1	Sheepshank: Step 2

Lay out two bights (see page xi) in the line in an S or Z shape.	Use the main line to tie two half hitches (see page 23) over the ends of both bights as shown in the photograph. Slowly pull on both the main parts of the line, taking care to keep the knot in its proper shape and form. The two loops at the ends of the knot need to stay approximately the same size.

Eye Splice

USED TO CREATE AN EYE AT THE END OF A ROPE

For sailors, being able to create an "eye," or a loop, at the end of a rope was once considered a basic and important skill. Although ropes with eyes can now be purchased, a reliable one can be made with this technique. It only works with laid ropes, and if the rope is hard-laid (see page 2) you will probably need a tool to work the strands apart. Tucking the strands three times works well with fiber ropes, but synthetic material, being slippery, requires five tucks to be secure. Finish the splice with tape, whipping, or heat (with synthetic material) to further secure it. This knot can also be useful to campers who need a permanent loop at the end of a rope.

Eye Splice: Step 1

Unlay the end of a rope (separate the strands) and form an eye of the required size. Tuck the end of one loose strand under a strand in the standing part. Tuck the next loose strand under the next strand in the standing part.

Eye Splice: Step 2

Turn the rope over and tuck the third loose strand under the only strand in the standing part that has yet to be used. Repeat the process until each loose strand has been tucked into the standing part three times. Roll the splice between your hands to achieve the proper shape.

113

Back Splice

A KNOT THAT INTERWEAVES THE STRANDS OF A LAID ROPE TO PREVENT FRAYING

Traditionally, ropes were made of three strands twisted (or laid) together. When the rope was cut to the required length, splicing was required to prevent fraying. Being able to back-splice a rope was considered a basic skill required of all sailors. Some ropes are made with four strands, but this same method of back splicing will work with four strands.

Since back splicing serves the same purpose as whipping (tying smaller stuff around a cut end of

Back Splice: Step 1	Back Splice: Step 2

Begin by interweaving the strands into a knot known as a crown, as shown in the photograph. Do this by forming a bight in each strand, then tucking the end of the adjacent strand through the bight. Work clockwise around the unraveled end of the rope.	Tighten the crown knot against the end of the rope. Splicing can start now.

rope to prevent fraying), this knot is sometimes known as Spanish whipping. Unlike whipping, a back splice actually becomes stronger with use. A similar interweaving of strands can be used to splice two ropes into one.

Back Splice: Step 3

Lead one strand against the lay of the rope (the direction of the twists of the strands). Go over the next strand and under the third strand. Do this with all three stands, making sure the strands leave the crown at regular intervals, each strand centered on approximately one-third of the circumference of the rope.

Back Splice: Step 4

Continue to weave the three stands against the lay of the rope, over and under, until each strand is tucked back into the rope two or three times. The strand ends may be trimmed off, but do not trim them too short, since the splice can un-ravel. Roll the splice between your hands to make it uniformly round.

Common Whipping

USED TO PREVENT A ROPE OF
SEVERAL STRANDS FROM FRAYING

Whipping is the process of wrapping and seizing the end of a rope or line with strong, thin twine to prevent fraying. A frayed end is difficult to use and eventually leads to loss of a section of a typically expensive rope. When a rope is to be cut, always take steps to prevent fraying before cutting. Synthetic twine should be used on synthetic rope and natural fiber twine on natural fiber ropes. The common whipping is far from the most secure whipping, but it will

Common Whipping: Step 1

Lay a loop (or bight) of twine along the rope near the end.

Common Whipping: Step 2

Wrap several turns of twine around the loop to bind it to the rope.

work until a dependable whipping, usually sewn, can be acquired. Some twines stretch when wet, allowing the whipping to slip off. Common whipping, therefore, requires retying occasionally until replaced. Campers and climbers may need to use whipping to prevent a cut rope from fraying.

Common Whipping: Step 3

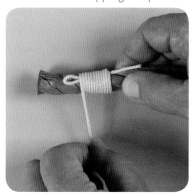

Continue binding the twine to the rope for a width at least a little greater than the diameter of the rope. Make the turns of twine as tight as possible.

Common Whipping: Step 4

Tuck the working end through what is left of the loop and tighten by pulling on the standing part until the loop disappears beneath the binding.

Asher's Bottle Sling

USED FOR HANGING A BOTTLE
OR OTHER SIMILAR CONTAINER
OF LIQUID

Onboard a ship, bottles of liquid—bottles of water, stove fuel, alcoholic beverages—can slip, slide, fall, spill, or break open. This is one of several sling knots that grip the necks of containers, glass bottle or otherwise, allowing the container to be hung safely aside or carried with greater ease. Asher's bottle sling is credited to Dr. Harry Asher and first appeared in print in *A New System of Knotting,* Volume 2, published in 1989.

Asher's Bottle Sling: Step 1

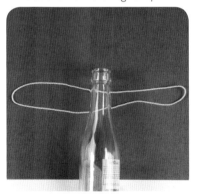

Begin by tying a piece of twine or cord into the appropriate-size loop. A fine knot for tying a loop is the double fisherman's knot (see page 90). Lay the loop beneath the neck of the bottle.

Asher's Bottle Sling: Step 2

Bring the bight on one side across the neck and through the bight on the other side, as shown in the photograph.

Sling knots may also be useful to anyone who wishes to secure a container of liquid for ease of carrying, hanging, or hauling. A climber, for instance, could use it to hang a water bottle from a climbing harness.

Asher's Bottle Sling: Step 3

Bring the outer bight across the neck and give it a half twist into a loop.

Asher's Bottle Sling: Step 4

Bring the inner bight under the neck of the bottle and through the loop. Tighten by pulling on the inner bight and adjust the whole knot until it seats acceptably against the neck.

119

Knife Lanyard Knot

THIS KNOT CREATES A FIXED LOOP FROM WHICH A KNIFE OR OTHER OBJECT CAN BE HUNG

Considering its simplicity, this is certainly one of the most attractive lanyard knots—and for that reason, one of the most often used. This knot was originally intended to create a fixed loop on a neck lanyard from which a seaman would suspend his knife. It can, of course, suspend many things and is known by other names, including the bosun's or boatswain's whistle knot, the pipe lanyard knot, and the two-strand diamond knot.

Knife Lanyard Knot: Step 1	Knife Lanyard Knot: Step 2

Drape the cord over your left hand as shown in the photo-graph. Make a loop in the end of the cord (as shown) and hold the loop between your thumb and index finger (as shown). Im-portant: The loop behind your hand will be the final loop.	Bring the end indicated in the photograph (the end hanging down to the left side in the step 1 photo) up through the loop in your palm as shown in the photograph.

Depending on the object to be hung from the lanyard, sometimes the item must be strung onto the cord prior to the tying of the knot. Sometimes the object can be tied to the fixed loop by way of a girth (or ring) hitch (see page 81). Enthusiasts will notice that this knot is a relative of the carrick bend. Though it appears complex to tie, it's really not that difficult; just have patience tightening the knot.

Knife Lanyard Knot: Step 3	Knife Lanyard Knot: Step 4

Bring the same end through the knot again as shown in the photograph.	Bring the other end through the knot as shown in the photograph. Slip the arrangement off your hand and meticulously work the knot into its final form.

121

Monkey's Fist

A LARGE, ROUND DECORATIVE KNOT WITH PRACTICAL USES

If you are imaginative, the monkey's fist (monkey fist, monkey paw) does resemble a fist. It may well be the most famous decorative knot, one recognized almost instantly by a vast number of people. It was probably developed by sailors who needed a heavy heaving line knot and who sometimes tied it around a stone or other spherical object to add weight. The knot can be tied around a rubber ball if flotation is desired.

Monkey's Fist: Step 1

Wrap the cord around your hand as shown in the photograph.

Monkey's Fist: Step 2

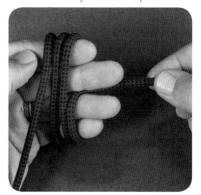

Trap the final wrap with your fingers as shown.

122

Decoratively, the monkey's fist is popular as a large and attractive end to any cord, especially if the cord will be used as a pull-string. It is most often tied as a two-ply or three-ply knot. (A three-ply knot is illustrated here.) It can be tied larger than a three-ply. In addition to being tied around a spherical object (a marble or golf ball would work fine for small jobs), it can be tied around your hand as a starting point; this is known as the sailor's method and is shown here.

Monkey's Fist: Step 3	Monkey's Fist: Step 4

Slip the upper half of the wraps off your fingers and continue to wrap an equal number of wraps around the first set of wraps, as shown in the photograph. A spherical object may be inserted at this point.	With the bundle entirely off your fingers, make a third set of wraps, the same in number, around and through where the two bundles of cord meet. It will take some time to tighten and form the ball into its final spherical shape. Be sure to tuck the end inside the knot to hide it.

Simple Chain Sinnet (Monkey Chain)

SUCCESSIVE LOOPS TUCKED NEATLY THROUGH ONE ANOTHER TO FORM A CHAIN

Chain sinnets, of which there are quite a few, have in common one or more strands that are formed into loops successively tucked into each other. A chain sinnet could be used to shorten a cord, as lanyard knots sometimes are, but this simple chain sinnet also creates the decorative gold braid seen on military uniform caps and shoulders. It is sometimes known as the trumpet cord, since it decorates the gold cord often dangling from military trumpets (or, more accurately, military bugles). It may also be called the monkey chain or the monkey braid.

Simple Chain Sinnet
(Monkey Chain): Step 1

Form a loop in the cord.

Simple Chain Sinnet
(Monkey Chain): Step 2

Tuck a second loop of the cord through the first loop as shown in the photograph. An over-hand with draw loop has now been tied in the cord.

The simple chain sinnet is the chain sinnet most often used in the world of knot tying. In addition to being decorative, it also serves, when tied loosely, as a method of packing short pieces of cord or rope in a manner that prevents tangling, a useful device for campers, climbers, and boaters. This method allows the cord or rope to be untied from the chain with ease. Once tied, the cord assumes an interesting elasticity.

Simple Chain Sinnet (Monkey Chain): Step 3

Tuck a third loop through the second loop. At this point begin to tighten and arrange the loops as you go along. *Note:* No tightening is necessary if the cord or rope is being prepared for packing or storage.

Simple Chain Sinnet (Monkey Chain): Step 4

Continue to add loops to the sinnet until you reach the desired length. Thread the working end through the final loop to lock the knot.

Figure 8 with follow through with double overhand.

INDEX

H

half hitch, 22
hangman's knot (noose), 20–21
hard-laid ropes, 2, 113
heat sealing, 3
heaving line knot, 8–9
hemp, 1
highwayman's hitch, 66–67
hitches, boat, 62–74
hitches, climbing, 78–86
hunter's (rigger's) bend, 87

I

interlocking loops, 109
International Guild of Knot Tyers, ix,
    11, 29, 31

J

joining lines, 44–49, 87–95
jute, 1

K

kernmantle, 2
killick hitch, 39
klemheist knot, 82
knife lanyard knot, 120–21

L

laid ropes, 2, 113, 114
leather, 1, 46
lines, 1
lines, joining, 44–49, 87–95
liquid whipping, 2
loop knot, 102
loops, boat, 50–61
loops, camping, 16–21

M

manila, 1
midshipman's hitch, 60–61
monkey chain, 124–25
monkey's fist, 122–23
moving hitches, camping, 34–39
Munter (Italian) hitch, 80

N

natural fibers, 1, 2, 12, 19, 33, 44
nomenclature, xii–xiii
noose, hangman's knot, 20–21
noose, simple, 19
nylon, 1, 51, 92

O

overhand knot, 6
overhand knot with draw loop, 7
overhand loop, 18

P

pile (post) hitch, 72
pole hitch, 70–71
polyethelene, 1, 46
polypropylene ropes, 1, 62
post hitch, 72
prusik knot, 84–85

R

reef knot, 13
rigger's bend, 87
ring hitch, 121
rolling hitch, 69
rope ends, 2, 3
ropes, 1–2
round turn & two half hitches, 86

ABOUT THE AUTHOR

Buck Tilton teaches at Central Wyoming College and is also the author of *Knack Knots You Need, Knack Hiking & Backpacking,* and *Knack First Aid.* His many books for FalconGuides, including the award-winning *Wilderness First Responder,* have sold more than 200,000 copies combined.